The Tower Menagerie

The Tower Menagerie

The Amazing 600-Year History of the
Royal Collection of Wild and Ferocious
Beasts Kept at the Tower of London

DANIEL HAHN

JEREMY P. TARCHER/PENGUIN
a member of Penguin Group (USA) Inc.
New York

Jeremy P. Tarcher/Penguin
a member of
Penguin Group (USA) Inc.
375 Hudson Street
New York, NY 10014
www.penguin.com

First Jeremy P. Tarcher/Penguin Edition 2004
First published in 2003 by Simon & Schuster UK, Ltd.

Library of Congress Cataloging-in-Publication Data

Hahn, Daniel, date.
The Tower menagerie : the amazing true story of the royal
collection of wild beasts / Daniel Hahn.
        p.   cm.
        ISBN 1-58542-335-1
    1. Menageries—England—London—History.
    2. Tower of London (London, England)—History.
                I. Title
QL73.G72L665   2004   2004041274
            590.73421'5—dc22

Printed in the United States of America
1   3   5   7   9   10   8   6   4   2

This book is printed on acid-free paper. ∞

Contents

List of Illustrations

Integrated

The chapter-head engravings are by William Harvey and are taken from E. T. Bennett's *The Tower Menagerie* (1829).

List of Illustrations

List of Illustrations

Plate section

1   Late-thirteenth-century fresco by Giotto showing St Francis in 1215 preaching to the famous flock of birds on the road from Cannara. SAN FRANCESCO UPPER CHURCH, ASSISI/BRIDGEMAN ART LIBRARY

2   Two images from the twelfth-century Worksop Bestiary. THE PIERPOINT MORGAN LIBRARY, NEW YORK

3   Detail from the late-thirteenth-century *Mappa Mundi* at Hereford Cathedral. COURTESY OF THE DEAN AND CHAPTER OF HEREFORD CATHEDRAL AND THE HEREFORD MAPPA MUNDI TRUST

4   *St George and the Dragon* by Paolo Uccello. THE NATIONAL GALLERY, LONDON

5   'Le Goût' (taste) from the tapestry sequence known as the *Dame à la Licorne*. MUSÉE NATIONAL DU MOYEN-AGE DE CLUNY, PARIS/RMN

6   'The Tyger' by William Blake, from his *Songs of Innocence and of Experience*. FITZWILLIAM MUSEUM, CAMBRIDGE

7   *The Great Indian Rhinoceros* by George Stubbs. THE ROYAL COLLEGE OF SURGEONS, LONDON

8   Fifteenth-century depiction of the White Tower from the poems of Charles, duke of Orléans. BRITISH LIBRARY

9   Early-fifteenth-century illumination by the Boucicaut Master showing Marco Polo arriving at the Gulf of Persia from India. BIBLIOTHÈQUE NATIONALE, PARIS/BRIDGEMAN ART LIBRARY

10   *John Tradescant the Younger*, 'in his Garden,' by Emanuel de Critz. ASHMOLEAN MUSEUM, OXFORD

11   *Giraffe*, watercolor believed to be by John Hunter. THE ROYAL COLLEGE OF SURGEONS, LONDON

12   *The Royal College of Surgeons Museum* by T. H. Shepherd. THE ROYAL COLLEGE OF SURGEONS, LONDON

13   *The Monkey Room* by Thomas Rowlandson. COURTESY OF DR ALAN BORG

List of Illustrations

Every effort has been made to trace copyright-holders; if copyright has been inadvertently infringed, please contact the publisher for corrections to be made to future editions.

Chronology of Reigns

HOUSE OF PLANTAGENET

John   1199–1216
Henry III   1216–1272
Edward I   1272–1307
Edward II   1307–1327
Edward III   1327–1377
Richard II   1377–1399

HOUSE OF LANCASTER

Henry IV   1399–1413
Henry V   1413–1422
Henry VI   1422–1461

HOUSE OF YORK

Edward IV   1461–1470
[Henry VI   1470–1471]
Edward IV   1471–1483
Edward V   1483
Richard III   1483–1485

Chronology of Reigns

HOUSE OF TUDOR

Henry VII   1485–1509
Henry VIII   1509–1547
Edward VI   1547–1553
Lady Jane Grey   1553
Mary   1553–1558
Elizabeth I   1558–1603

HOUSE OF STUART

James I   1603–1625
Charles I   1625–1649
Commonwealth   1649–1660

HOUSE OF STUART (RESTORED)

Charles II   1660–1685
James II   1685–1688
William III   1689–1702 (with Mary to 1694)
Anne   1702–1714

HOUSE OF HANOVER

George I   1714–1727
George II   1727–1760
George III   1760–1811
Regency   1811–1820
George IV   1820–1830
William IV   1830–1837
Victoria   1837–1901

Preface

When building work began on the Tower of London during the reign of William the Conqueror, London was hardly bigger than a small town, with a few thousand inhabitants, their houses, their means of livelihood and little else. Nine centuries later the Tower still stands. Now a symbol of continuity, above all, it has in its long history symbolized oppression and terror, or royal grandeur and pomp, or a very particular perspective on English history and historical heritage; it has been a prison, a mint, the home to a garrison, a massive arsenal, a repository of the public records, an occasional royal household and latterly a hugely successful tourist operation.

For most of its existence the Tower also housed the Royal Menagerie, the collection of wild and not-so-wild animals that the country's kings and queens found themselves lumbered with following acts of misplaced generosity by well-intentioned foreign potentates. Of all the strands of the Tower's history, this is the least familiar (I only learned of it myself a couple of years ago, and then quite by accident), and yet it has turned out also to be one of the most entertaining and revealing. Hence this book, an attempt to tell the story of the Menagerie, but also to use this story to explore myriad other subjects. The Menagerie is the prism, if you like, for examining many things, whether the birth of modern surgery, developments in artistic technique, the rise of journalism, our changing perceptions of animals and the natural world, or (of course) the stories of the Tower itself and its fortunate and less fortunate inhabitants.

This approach is not without its problems. The story of the Royal Menagerie is a rather unwieldy one; as I wrote this book I sometimes felt as though the narrative covered more centuries and disciplines than it was perhaps sensible to undertake in a single short work. The historical scope – six centuries and more – is itself more than a little daunting. When this particular story begins, the capital was only a fraction of the size of today's London; it still all fell within the Roman wall, with the Tower sitting at the eastern end, and Ludgate at the west – the walk from one end of the city to the other would have taken under half an hour. Since the construction of the Tower had begun a hundred and fifty years earlier the population of the city had risen, but only to about ten thousand. The great crusader Richard 'the Lionheart' had only lately died, some few years earlier. The English had ventured across the Channel to Europe, but beyond Europe – who could say what might lie there? What strange countries and people and frightening beasts might be found towards the edges of the (flat) earth? By the time the Menagerie closed in the 1830s the city was all but unrecognizable. The Industrial Revolution was coming to an end, the population had rocketed to close to two million, twenty-nine monarchs had come and gone, and the young Princess Victoria was just about to accede to the throne. The world was a far, far bigger place, and Britain owned much of it.

As a work of history, this book makes a claim to cover a good amount of the intervening ground by exploring what happened in that time. It is not, however, a completely chronological work of history; not all of the material is in the right order, and I've made all sorts of links between periods and disciplines in an attempt to convey the texture of the subject, its chaotic nature and its importance, rather than merely its bare chronology. Chapter 1, for instance, covers the first half-century or so of the Menagerie's existence, but it includes a story about a polar bear in the Thames, an eyewitness account of a dragon fight, some heraldry, some Pliny the Elder and quite a bit of serious 'which king did what when' history; chapter 7, purporting to examine the Tower Menagerie at the close of the eighteenth century, is also about grave-robbing and theology and surgery and has quotations from Byron's wife and a fictional Chinese encyclopedia; and so on. The random-seeming connections between subjects and events, within and between chapters, do I think reflect the nature of the Menagerie's story. For it is not simply a history of how 'a lion came, it died, a polar bear came, then an elephant came, then the polar bear died, then two more lions came, one of them died . . .' Fortunately it is not like that at all. Rather the contrary, since at one point or other the Menagerie influenced and was affected by almost every strand of cultural, scientific and political life during the six centuries of its existence. You will find this peculiar story winding its course through literature, painting, philosophy, theology and superstition, through English history, of course, and animal rights, through politics and political satire, treason, natural history, surgery and more.

All of which is more than enough to be getting along with, without also attempting to propose a thesis on the role of zoos, on their great value or inherent evil, on their present and future. But it is also arguable that in this enlightened day it would be cowardly to tell the story of a zoo without attempting to address this question in some way, to acknowledge the importance of the question, at least, even if no claim is made to answering it.

It is unquestionable that the best-run zoos – and without hesitation I number the Menagerie's direct descendant, London Zoo, among these – do fulfil very valuable functions of education and conservation. What is in question is whether these functions outweigh the necessary losses (they can of course only be fulfilled at the expense of their captives' liberty and ability to lead 'natural' lives). So the old debate on animal rights continues – not, these days, on whether animals should have rights at all, of course, but on what exactly these rights should consist of. It is, after all, through this question of rights that, in England at least, the progress of humanity with respect to its relations with animals is measured. There are plans under way in the government to draft a document tantamount to an Animal Bill of Rights. In the United States, the Federal Animal Welfare Act provides limited protection for lab animals. All well and good. But does such legislation go far enough? Should animals perhaps be afforded rights comparable to what we consider to be fundamental *human* rights? Should they, in other words, be automatically entitled not just to lives free from cruelty and abuse but to the great gift of Liberty itself? Or is the difference between a chimpanzee and his close cousin Man significant enough to justify certain behavior towards one that would be considered quite unacceptable if inflicted on the other?

I cannot claim to be an expert in conservation issues, in today's captivity conditions, in animal law, animal behavior or neurosciences, and I have no real insights that would make a satisfactory answer; I can offer only a personal view, which is instinctive and honest, but also deeply ambivalent. It is ambivalent because I find myself – not a little surprised – with a sentimental attachment to London Zoo and the idea of zoos, while at the same time being convinced by the utterly persuasive arguments against them. Hence the dilemma that I suspect many people face.

The tension is best expressed, I think, with words from the much maligned Lord Shelburne, the little-known eighteenth-century independent prime minister, who wrote in a memoir that

> it requires no small labour to open the eyes of either the public or an individual, but when that is accomplished you have not got a third of the way. The real difficulty remains in getting people to apply the principles which they have admitted and of which they are now so fully convinced. Then springs the mine composed of private interests and personal animosity.

So in spite of all that conviction I might feel about animals' rights, all those powerful arguments, the inevitable 'mine of private interests' may be more powerful still.

Looking back to Henry III and his leopards, though, I can at least be glad at the great progress that *has* been made, the improvements that *have* been secured, gradually over these many centuries. Although some people would seek to speed this progress up, some few others to slow it down, I have no doubt at least that we are moving in the right direction.

Preface

*

As a consequence of the multidisciplinary nature of this book, and its historical scope, I have had to rely on the expertise and generosity of dozens of people – literally – who know far more about each of its distinct subjects than I ever will. There's a famous scene in *The Adventures of Tom Sawyer* where Tom has been set to do some whitewashing by his Aunt Polly, and by persuading his friends how much fun he's having, he fools them into doing all the hard work for him. And but for the fact that Tom's friends paid him to help, while I wasn't able to persuade any of mine to go quite that far, my job in writing this book has often felt like Tom's afternoon whitewashing that fence. Those many generous enough to let themselves be gulled into doing all the hard work (while I traipsed happily around Britain, France, Italy, Ireland and Germany, often for no very good reason) include the following.

Jeremy Ashbee at the Tower took great time and trouble to answer numerous queries of all kinds over the last months of writing; Simon Chaplin of the Hunterian Museum answered my questions about John Hunter; Phillip Thomas found me a reference on James I; Troy Bickham told me all sorts of useful and interesting things about mastodons; Neil Hanson answered a query about the Great Fire; Graham Keevill and the Oxford Archaeological Unit provided information about the dig they undertook of the Menagerie site; Jeremy Osborn provided information and answers about the British Empire in general and the East India Company in particular; and a last-minute intervention in the form of a letter from Claire Tomalin prevented me from making an embarrassing mistake in the section on Samuel Pepys.

Preface

The staffs of the British Library, the London Library, the libraries of the Zoological Society of London and Trinity College, Dublin, and the Public Record Office were unfailingly helpful and tolerant. Thanks are also due to Bridget Clifford, the senior curator of the Tower's library, for putting her resources and knowledge at my disposal.

While working on her fine biography of Arbella Stuart, Sarah Gristwood came across several anecdotes of visits to the Menagerie that she kindly brought to my notice; Enrique Walker drew my attention to Borges's Chinese encyclopedia and gave me information about Bentham's Panopticon; Abigail Anderson found the link to the Gordon Riots; Peter Holmes sent me the folk song that appears as the epigraph to chapter 6, and introduced me to the 'lions i' th' Tower' reference in Webster's *The White Devil*; Mark Hamilton brought a seventeenth-century description of Menagerie animals to my attention; Deirdre Le Faye very kindly wrote to inform me of the link to Jane Austen; and Jo Feather found me a reference to the Menagerie in a recent novel. All these discoveries and observations I have plundered for my own use and included in this book.

The Tower Menagerie has been read at various stages by a number of people whose specific and general comments have gone a long way towards making it a far better thing than it once was. Becky Swift was instrumental at the earliest stages, helping me pull together the chaotic ideas of the project's inception into something that might eventually become a reasonably sensible book. Among those who subsequently read it, in part or as a whole (sometimes more than once), I should thank Iannis Carras, Tanweena Chowdhury, Daniela de Groote, Ilan Feder, Leonie

Flynn, Sara Goulden, Candida Gray, Laura Hutchings, Yzanne Mackay, Leon Menezes, Susan Posner, James Reynolds and Rebecca Tomasini. The input of all of these to early or late drafts was invaluable.

Of those who read drafts I would in particular like to thank Chris Bazley, Paul Kassabian and Chester Omana for their comments and help. Chris dealt with many of the inaccuracies of my overenthusiastic and amateurish practices, expressing his outrage at my inexcusable assumptions and generalizations with consistent delicacy and politeness – he is a proper historian at heart, and I have to thank him, as well as Jeremy Osborn and Iannis Carras (both, likewise, more natural scholars than I will ever be), for letting an amateur like me get away with it. Paul served as the model for my ideal reader, and his thoughts about what was and was not interesting about the book have to a great extent shaped what it has become. Chester provided invaluable comments on two drafts (making them at once more accurate and more interesting) and has throughout the process provided new thoughts and ways of looking at the subject; I have in many cases been guided by his ideas (and in others have simply stolen them wholesale), and they have made this book far better and more ambitious than it was before he began to think about it for me.

With all that help there seemed hardly anything left for me to do; but if there are inadequacies and inaccuracies in the book they fall in the small areas between my friends' great contributions, and needless to say the fault for these remains with me.

Araminta Whitley, my agent, and Celia Hayley of Lucas Alexander Whitley coordinated the important transition between quite-a-good-idea-I-once-had and something-that-would-one-day-be-a-real-book, for which I cannot be too grateful. My editor, Andrew Gordon, was not only good enough to take a risk in buying the thing to begin with, he then followed through to ensure it would be a far better book than I could have conceived of without his help. Throughout the process he has curbed my worst excesses, told me what I could and couldn't get away with, and politely crossed out my less-than-subtle (and possibly less-than-funny) jokes with endless patience and good grace. Ashley Shelby negotiated the tricky process of preparing the text for an American edition with sensitivity and patience; my thanks to her, too, for making this potentially tiresome process a pleasure.

Finally, and most of all, I must thank my family, my various parents and siblings of all kinds. It will come as no surprise to anyone who knows them to learn that they were an inexhaustible source of support of every kind during the researching and writing of this book. I could not have done it without them. In particular, anyone who knows her will know that my sister Emily is, simply, amazing. This book is dedicated to her.

DANIEL HAHN
London, 2002

The Tower
Menagerie

Prologue

On 31 December 1764, a lean, elderly man made his way through the western entrance into the Tower of London. He was small and white-locked, talkative and charismatic, and probably wore a cassock and clerical collar under his winter cloak (he was, after all, a man of God). Accompanying him was another man, unprepossessing, carrying a small boxwood flute.

The two men did not venture far into the fortress complex, however; they stopped instead at the small custom-built island partway along the entrance causeway. It was here that the king's animals were kept, and it was these residents of the great Tower that the two men had braved the cold to come and see.

The preacher was the sixty-one-year-old John Wesley (responsible with his brother for the founding of the Methodist Church), and he had brought along his flute-playing acquaintance in order to conduct a sort of spiritual test.

A tireless traveler, Wesley continued to journey thousands of miles a year, usually on horseback, into his late eighties, preaching a staggering forty thousand sermons over the course of his long life. In this instance he had recently returned from a visit to Scotland where he witnessed the strangely hypnotic effect music had had on a lion there.[*] So once back in London, 'I thought it would be worth while to make an odd experiment. Remembering how surprisingly fond of music the lion at Edinburgh was, I went to the Tower with one who plays on the German flute.'

By watching the reactions of these animals, he thought, it might be possible to ascertain whether or not they possessed souls.[†] The results of the experiment, as he goes on to describe, are peculiar, though, it must be said, hardly conclusive: 'He began playing near four or five lions; only one of these rose up, came to the front of his den, and seemed to be all attention. Meantime, a tiger leaped over the lion's back, turned and ran under his belly, leaped over him again, and so to and fro incessantly.'

One can only guess what the Menagerie's other visitors that

---

[*] In the summer of 2000 I spent a couple of days in Edinburgh, trying (unsuccessfully, as it turned out) to trace this animal; it became clear quite quickly that there was no record of a lion having been anywhere in the city during this period. My best lead in the search took me to Hopetoun House, a magnificent stately home some dozen miles outside the city. The archivist there had no record of the house ever having had a lion in it. 'But,' she said hopefully, 'we did have an emu once for a bit. Would that help?'

[†] Many people have commented on the power of music to bring out a creature's essential humanity. Lenin once wrote that he had stopped listening to Beethoven, since he found that the music had tended to soften his nature excessively, making him unable to be as single-minded as he would have liked. Oliver Goldsmith was only one of those who recognized intelligent animals' capacity to appreciate music. In his *History of the Earth and Animated Nature* (1774) he observed how one particular elephant seemed 'delighted with music.'

afternoon must have thought of the spectacle, this respectable-looking man of the cloth appearing to charm these wild animals into the most peculiar and undignified behavior.

Even Wesley could find no explanation for the animals' reactions, but for the possibility that they had some kind of divine soul moving them to react as they did: 'Can we account for this by any principle of mechanism? Can we account for it at all?'

Wesley's experiences in Edinburgh and at the Tower had merely served to revive and refocus a question that had concerned him for some years:

> What is the barrier between men and brutes? [he had asked
> some years earlier] . . . What is the line which they cannot
> pass? It was not reason. Set aside that ambiguous term:
> exchange it for the plain word, understanding; and who can
> deny that brutes have this? We may as well deny that they
> have sight or hearing.

It was a sign of this divinity – not merely reason or 'understanding' – that Wesley was looking for in the animals' responses to music. Although it was still widely assumed at the time that animals were neither particularly spiritual nor indeed even capable of great understanding, the question had been raised frequently and regularly since antiquity. Pythagoras's and Plato's belief in metempsychosis, the transmigration of souls after death between humans, birds and animals, was well known in England a century and a half before Wesley's experiment. In Shakespeare's *Twelfth Night*, first performed back in 1602, Feste had questioned Malvolio about Pythagoras's views in a warped test of Malvolio's sanity:

FESTE: What is the opinion of Pythagoras concerning wild
    fowl?
MALVOLIO: That the soul of our grandam might haply
    inhabit a bird.
FESTE: What thinkest thou of his opinion?
MALVOLIO: I think nobly of the soul and in no way approve
    his opinion.

In Feste's topsy-turvy world it is Malvolio's (Christian) refusal to agree with Pythagoras that confirms his insanity: 'Thou shalt hold the opinion of Pythagoras ere I will allow of thy wits, and fear to kill a woodcock, lest thou dispossess the soul of thy grandam. Fare thee well.'

Even within the Christian tradition the poor prospects of animals' survival *post mortem* was not universally assumed. And although it must be said that the prevalent view among preachers and divines until the eighteenth century was that animals were entirely physical and nondivine, there are notable exceptions. Foremost among our cultural references, of course, is St Francis of Assisi, an exemplary Christian and devout nature-lover who famously preached to a flock of birds assembled on the road from Cannara in 1215. St Francis's audience, unlike Wesley's manic tiger, did not react in any very animated way,* but Francis was pleasantly surprised that at least they retained the good grace not

---

* According to Francis's biographer, Thomas of Celano, they sat there 'stretching their necks, spreading their wings and opening their beaks and gazing at him.' Thomas optimistically considered this behavior 'remarkable.'

to fly away. The chronicler Roger of Wendover, writing shortly after St Francis's canonization in 1228, suggested rather uninspiringly that this may have been due to the presence of a fresh and juicy dead body in the vicinity, rather than the engaging glow of redemption the birds could sense in the preaching of the great man (though it is the latter explanation that makes for the more heartening story).

As it happens it was just around this time, while St Francis was carrying out his roadside experiments on the imperturbable birds on the other side of Europe, that the story of Wesley's lions really begins. For the big cats Wesley had come to visit in the Tower of London were only the latest inhabitants of the Royal Menagerie there, the latest in a line stretching back a full five centuries and more, to the early years of the thirteenth century.

Henry III, the fourth Plantagenet king, was on the English throne.

I

Royal Gifts

The story really begins, then, in late February 1235, with the announcement that Isabella, the English king's sister, is to marry Frederick II, Holy Roman Emperor.

The charismatic Frederick – scholar, patron of the arts and military hero – was known throughout Europe as *stupor mundi*, 'the wonder of the world.' Like Henry back in England, Frederick was an exceptionally cultured man; unlike Henry he was also widely admired and widely feared. He was also, arguably, the most powerful man in the world.

A contemporary Franciscan monk, Salimbene, wrote of him in his *Chronicle*:

He was crafty, wily, avaricious, lustful, malicious, wrathful; and yet a gallant man at times, when he would show his kindness or courtesy; full of solace, jocund, delightful, fertile in devices. He knew to read, write, and sing, and to make songs and music. . . . Moreover, he knew to speak with many and varied tongues, and, to be brief, if he had been rightly Catholic, and had loved God and His Church, he would have had few emperors his equal in the world.

Though he was not much of a Catholic, this grand Emperor Frederick did at least like a good spectacle, so there was no question in anybody's mind but that the wedding at Worms Cathedral would be an ostentatiously lavish affair. And in the event no one was disappointed. Besides the chance to feast on such a scale 'that more could not be imagined,' Frederick took the opportunity to bring with him to Worms a selection of animals from his private menageries to be paraded through the town for his and his guests' entertainment.

Worms Cathedral was (is) an unusual building, and a curious choice for a ceremony of this kind. Like its counterpart in Durham, a cathedral town in the north of England, it has no great door at its western end, which would not have made it easy to make a grand entrance with a spectacular procession.* Especially if one is hoping to process with very large numbers of very large animals. And to make it more awkward still, the town of Worms

---

* By the east window, incidentally, there are a series of fantastic animal carvings, depicting monkeys, lions devouring men, and all sorts of other delights. They were already there, in fact, though then quite new, when Isabella, Frederick and the royal zoo arrived in 1235 for the big event.

was at that time in a state of siege (Frederick's wayward son was responsible for this). None of which appears to have got in Frederick's way, and on 22 July the marriage somehow went ahead as planned, processing animals and all.

To celebrate the union with Isabella and with England, Frederick generously decided to give his new brother-in-law Henry three of the magnificent wildcats from his beloved collection. These elegant animals (a flattering reference to the three on Henry's crest) arrived on the Kent coast later that year. They were called 'leopards.'

Wildcats had been on the Royal Arms of the English kings since the appearance on the scene of Geoffrey Plantagenet and his family in the previous century; but whatever Frederick may have thought, these creatures were not leopards but lions. Henry's uncle, the famous lion-hearted king Richard I, had used the three Plantagenet lions passant[*] on his crest (Richard was Geoffrey's grandson). The three lions have remained on the Royal Arms ever since, though over the years they have been quartered with other emblems depending on the state of the territories – with Scotland's proud-defiant lion rampant[†] and the Irish harp (both incorporated by James I and VI), or French fleurs-de-lys (introduced by Edward III, a man with a political point to make). Alongside the lion-and-unicorn the three lions passant are still the English component in the crest, and it is these three that feature

---

[*] Walking on four legs, not raised on their hind legs.
[†] Raised up on its hind legs (as in a lion-and-unicorn crest).

on the England team's football shirt, as the famous team song so proudly affirms.

For someone living in the thirteenth century, making reference to a three-lion crest through a gift comprising three leopards (and no lions) would have been an excusable mistake. For one thing, the word 'leopard' was used almost synonymously with the word 'lion,' and to add to the confusion any lions not rampant were called, in French, *léopards* – this would of course have applied to the three on Henry's Plantagenet crest. Besides which, stylized heraldic lions do not bear the greatest resemblance to living lions, and the distinction cannot have been easy to draw if you had not had the opportunity to see either one of the species for yourself.* An easy enough mistake to make.

In any case, the association with the Plantagenet crest was a good excuse for a generous gift of this kind; and Frederick probably wouldn't have needed much prompting anyway. After all, there was a grand and venerable tradition of grand and powerful people giving grand animals to other grand and powerful people. Frederick could only benefit from being associated with potentates of that kind (so, for that matter, could Henry). So over the animals came – and whatever species these three wildcats were, they were doubtless a source of great pride to the court. And on

---

* Given this confusion, I should point out that it is not beyond the bounds of possibility that Frederick did in fact correctly give Henry three lions and not three leopards, that it was the chroniclers who were mistaken, and not the emperor.

went the tradition of the great kings of antiquity who had shown their power, their nobility and their great worldliness by displaying such rare and fabulous creatures for their impressionable people (and, more importantly, their impressionable foreign visitors) to wonder at. And at this point in his reign (as indeed throughout it) Henry's reputation and authority needed all the help they could get.

Having assumed the throne as a young child, Henry had only recently succeeded in wresting power away from his magnates, and was still – as he was to be throughout his long reign – a weak king, unpopular and distrusted. The old social order based on feudal rights and duties was still intact, and the power of the nobility had been strengthened in the Magna Carta, signed by his father (the even more unpopular King John) in 1215; this decentralization meant that without the support of his nobles (and he was under no illusion about how little support he could count on from such quarters) Henry had little effective power.

In the absence of a significant military victory over the French (always a favorite popularity boost for unpopular English kings), the best Henry could have wished for was an impressive foreign union, which he found in his sister's marriage to Frederick; when Frederick's counselor Peter de Vinea came over to England to broker the deal Henry must have been thrilled. Besides, not only was he gaining this new, impressive, imperial brother-in-law, but with him came a splendid gift that showed England what a magnificent and worldly king they had – and, into the bargain, one for whom even distrusting foreigners could find respect. (And besides this, in addition to his animal gifts, Frederick promised to help Henry against the forces of the French if required. Leopards were all very well, but help beating the French was a truly useful wedding present.)

When the time came, then, to receive charge of his three new beasts, Henry would have sought counsel from his advisors. For some reason it was decided that the animals should be kept in London (perhaps for ease of showing off) rather than sent to one of the many rather more spacious estates outside the city. So for lack of any better solution the animals were given a makeshift home in the Tower of London, William the Conqueror's great fortress on the north bank of the Thames. Henry had already begun a massive program of expanding and improving the Tower, a program that over the course of his reign was to cost him some £9,000.* This was to include the whitewashing (in 1241) of the famous central building, the great stone keep that subsequently came to be known as the White Tower, the name it has kept to this day.

Henry himself lived at the Tower only rarely; when he did it was usually because he had something disagreeable to escape from, so he invested in security in the form of a new curtain wall enclosing the Tower complex around its three land sides, a water-filled moat and so on. His own residence was in the brand-new Wakefield Tower, the construction of which ate up a large amount of the remainder of the budget. He rebuilt the Great Hall and spent money on costly new decoration and new windows. By the end of his reign the Tower would be a more

---

* Something like $11–12 million today.

comfortable and more impressive place in which to spend his days, albeit only occasional days. And now, in 1235, it also came to house the Royal Leopard Collection.

As one might expect, no one in Henry's permanent staff at the Tower had the least notion of how to deal with these three new additions to the household; nor indeed did William de Botton, the unfortunate man appointed by Henry to keep an eye on them. It comes as no surprise to learn that they did not last long (the leopards, not the staff). By August 1237, there are accounts relating to expenses for 'two of the king's leopards'; there is then an entry in 1240 that might be a reference to just a single leopard; and after that, silence.

It was not an auspicious beginning.

It could be argued that de Botton and his fellows should have known better. After all, it was not as if this were the first such collection – indeed, it was not even the first in the country. Henry's great-grandfather, the first king of that name (and youngest son of the Tower-building William the Conqueror), had been the first English monarch to keep a private collection of animals, which he housed at Woodstock, just outside Oxford. Here, according to the chronicler William of Malmesbury, Henry had taken delight in assembling 'lions, leopards, lynxes, camels, animals which England does not produce . . . He had placed there also a creature called a porcupine, sent to him by William of Montpelier.' This odd beast, one of Henry's favorites, was apparently 'an animal covered with bristly hairs which it naturally darts against the dog when pursuing it.' Furthermore, 'the bristles which I have seen are more than a span long, sharp at each extremity, like the quills of a goose where the feather ceases, but rather thicker, and speckled, as it were, with black and white.' The presence of these animals at Woodstock helps to explain why in about 1110 King Henry decided he wanted a high wall built around the perimeter of the gardens there.

There is a record of another animal, a camel, sent by Frederick to Henry in the same year as the three leopards, 'as a sign of his unceasing affection' (according to chronicler Matthew Paris); but as there is no record of its arriving at the Tower or residing there, we can assume that it was brought instead to Woodstock. Unless of course it simply died on the road and didn't make it anywhere at all, which is not unlikely.

Anyone hoping to find traces of Woodstock and its old Menagerie today is in for a disappointment, albeit a very grand-looking one. The site was built over in the early eighteenth century; big, barnlike, medieval Woodstock was replaced by vast, magnificent Blenheim Palace. Blenheim is one of the most impos-ing, showy, stately homes in the country, overpowering enough that it doesn't reveal even the faintest echo of its Woodstock days to the twenty-first-century visitor. The gardens have been land-scaped, ruthlessly, out of all recognition by 'Capability' Brown and others, and the old perimeter wall torn down. The wall had been necessary to keep the animals contained (both those exotic beasts for viewing and showing off and those more expendable ones for hunting), and to prevent curious peasants from being drawn to gape at the animals, or pawing important guests – today, of course, they have very efficient security staff and no doubt a system of closed-circuit television cameras too. So all that remains of Woodstock, beneath the sculpted hedges and landscaped waterfalls and gilded doorways and neoclassical columns and artificial lakes, is the plateau on which it sits and the distinctive rolling of the landscape around it.

Even in the days of Henry I the keeping of exotic animals by royalty or nobility was hardly a new idea; rather it had its roots as far back as classical antiquity, which helped to give it not just respectability, but a certain continental *je ne sais quoi*, and something of the Ancients' kudos. After all, hadn't Ptolemy II of Egypt celebrated his accession by processing in triumph through the streets of Alexandria with a convoy of chariots drawn by elephants, antelope, buffaloes, ostriches and zebras? (There's even a legend that when the Emperor Claudius arrived in Britain in AD 43, he came ashore on one of his elephants so as better to impress the locals.) And hadn't Pliny the Elder used visits to the private zoos of wealthy Romans in his studies for his *Natural History*? (Among other gems, this research led Pliny to discover that, according to one imaginative translator, chameleons become enraged when placed in fig trees.) And even Philip of Macedon and his son Alexander the Great had taken the time – between conquests – to amass a magnificent collection of exciting foreign beasts at vast expense to send back to Alexander's teacher Aristotle. More extraordinary still, Aristotle used them to write what is considered the first book of systematic natural history. Unusually for his time (as indeed it would have been even in the time of Henry III), Aristotle's interest in the animals sent to him was not merely the unquestioning wonder of a tourist, a showoff collector or a halfhearted amateur naturalist, but was far more curious, questioning and – to use an entirely anachronistic word – *scientific*. Apart from a handful of isolated exceptions, focused scientific interests of this kind (pursued with any sort of conviction) were not known in England until well after the Renaissance, with the work of the first experimenters of the dawning Enlightenment.

But even without any sign of the first zoologists, animals themselves there most certainly were. In fact, not only were Frederick's leopards not the first royal captive animals in England, but strictly speaking they may not even have been the first such collection in the Tower. For centuries, stories of the Menagerie have begun, as this one has done, with Frederick's gift to Henry III. Recent evidence has shown, however, that it may in fact have been Henry's father, King John, who first kept a private collection of animals in the Tower. Although we have no explicit record of the presence of animals there during that time, there are mysterious accounts in 1210 and the following couple of years of payments to John FitzHugh, the constable of the Tower, relating to the wages of the lion-keepers. King John had certainly brought foreign and exotic animals back to England in 1204 (three full crateloads). This was the year he finally lost Normandy; he retreated with just the collection of wild beasts as a memento – not a great deal, however much you may like animals.

And yet even with these three decades' experience, the keepers at the Tower under Henry III seem to have been highly doubtful as to how best to look after their bewildering charges.

The Emperor Frederick, on the other hand, could probably have taught Henry and his keepers a thing or two; he was something of an authority on animals, with not one but three extensive private zoos. Many of their grander inhabitants – elephants, camels, monkeys, leopards – occasionally made up a sort of scratch traveling menagerie to keep their owner amused during his long travels (it is impossible, of course, to overestimate the importance of keeping the emperor amused) and were among those that put in an appearance at his wedding to Isabella. In November 1233 he had traveled to Ravenna, taking lions, elephants, panthers, camels and other assorted beasts with him; on his trip to Verona in 1245 he had an elephant, five leopards and no fewer than two dozen camels. Frederick also kept a giraffe (which he had swapped with al-Kamil, the sultan of Egypt, for a polar bear) and, with rather more initiative than Henry managed to show on behalf of his animals, had set up a training school for cheetahs. Besides this, he was an expert falconer and had recently completed an illustrated book on the subject; this six-volume work, *The Art of Hunting with Birds*, was much praised when it first appeared – though that in itself is perhaps unsurprising, its author being who he was – and (more surprising) remains in print today.*

And Frederick was not alone. By the time Henry III and his three leopards laid the (metaphorical) foundation stone for the Menagerie in the Tower in 1235, private – and usually royal – menageries were quite commonplace around Europe.

---

* Incidentally, in a moment of extraordinary zeal (though admittedly by no means extraordinary for him), St Francis of Assisi once sought an audience with Frederick (who by another coincidence was baptized in the same font in Assisi as Francis), with the ambitious hope of persuading him to give up falconry and other similar mistreatments and objectifications of God's creatures. It is a curious thought that had this audience been granted and Francis achieved his aim, the story of the Tower Menagerie might never have made it past King John and the poor spoils of his crusades.

Frederick's leopards were soon followed into the Tower by a lion; where this animal may have come from we do not know, but there are records in March 1240 of a writ relating to the maintenance of 'the King's lion':

> March 23, 1240. To the sheriffs of London. *Contrabreve* to find the King's Lion and his keeper their necessities, as long as they shall be in the Tower of London. To the same, *contrabreve* to cause the said William the keeper of the King's Lion, to have 14 shillings that he expended in buying chains and other things for the use of the Lion.

It has been suggested that this actually refers to one of Frederick's leopards who against the odds had survived these five years. Besides that confusing interchangeability of the words 'lion' and 'leopard,' there is still the more suggestive question: with these animals among the first of their kind in London, if not the very first, who could realistically be expected to tell which was which?

But after this mysterious arrival (if new arrival it was), and the frenzy of the early years, the Menagerie went quiet for some time; indeed this animal, new lion or old leopard, would have had to keep the flag flying quite alone for over a decade. All this changed in 1252 when the king decided to liven things up a little at his great fortress on the Thames by having his old family collection from Woodstock brought down to London.

Even now, at the start of the twenty-first century, with the benefit of motorized transport, cranes, mechanical winches and the like, moving large and ferocious animals across the country is no easy task. It is daunting to imagine how much harder still it would have been for the keeper at Woodstock to crate and transport the lynxes, camels, leopards and lions the sixty miles down the London Road (now the relatively civilized M40), without so much as a stun-gun or a sedative for emergencies. Just keeping the animals calm as their huge crates were loaded onto the backs of the carts must have been fraught, to say the least. A lion can weigh up to 551 pounds, so the lifting alone would have been no small struggle. And then there was the terrible, interminable ride down that bumpy old road, with – riding along just behind – a number of very large wildcats beginning to get restless, and just a bit irritable.

Although this move meant that the Woodstock keeper was in danger of losing his livelihood, he must have breathed a sigh of relief when the operation was over, the crates unloaded, the animals settled into their new homes, and their keeping passed into the hands of His Majesty's London man, probably still our William de Botton.

And still greater excitement for de Botton was to follow on the heels of this massive move, with a new arrival that was no less exciting than Frederick's leopards (which, while not much use in battle against the French, were at least attractive and gratifyingly ferocious). There must suddenly have been plenty around the place to keep Mr de Botton busy.

It was 1252. A university had just been founded in the little market town of Oxford; Albertus Magnus was in Cologne, preparing himself to embark on compiling his massive zoological treatise, the twenty-six-volume *De Animalibus*; in Venice the Polos would soon be expecting the birth of their son Marco; just outside London to the west work had begun on the magnificent building that was to be Westminster Abbey. Norway at this time was being ruled by King Håkon IV, a decisive, stubborn king, a man who in his time had united his kingdom, annexed Greenland and Iceland, and in 1241 ordered the assassination of the Icelandic literary historian Snorri Sturluson (thereby single-handedly bringing to an end our primary means of access to an entire tradition of old Norse literature). This mixed blessing of a monarch was one man who did hold England's King Henry in high esteem. He chose to show this respect by presenting Henry with the gift of a 'pale bear.' This may or may not have been a polar bear; but medieval records being what they are (and medieval taxonomy of species being more rudimentary and haphazard still), there is unfortunately no categorical evidence that a polar bear is what it was, rather than a white strain of black bear.* The fact that the people of London seemed so surprised by the appearance of this animal, though, does suggest that it was significantly different from the numerous brown bears then roaming the island. We cannot be sure, however. In 1252 King Henry addressed a letter to 'the keeper of our pale bear, lately sent us from Norway, and which is in our Tower of London'; and that one word, 'pale' (or 'white,' depending on your translation), is the only reference we have to the animal's color. If this was in fact a polar bear (the most likely case, besides being the more appealing idea), it was the first seen in England – indeed one of only a

---

* 'Brown bears' can only ever be brown. 'Black bears,' rather eccentrically, can be found in both black and white.

handful before the arrival of the great Samson* at London Zoo
in 1829.

This unprecedentedly awkward gift arrived in London with
its keeper in the autumn of 1252. And – polar bear or not – it
certainly lost no time in capturing the attention and imagination
of the people of the city.

At first the sheriffs of the City of London were asked (told) to
provide money towards the animal's food and keep (they did so,
dutifully, though the 4 sous† a day they provided were barely sufficient); but after a year or so of this expense, albeit a rather
ungenerous, rather meagre expense, the people of London were
wisely instructed to invest in a muzzle, chain and rope, so that the
animal could be kept on the bank of the Thames and could fish for
his own food.

> Greetings. We command you that for the keeper of our white
> bear, recently arrived from Norway . . . ye cause to be had
> one muzzle and one iron chain to hold that bear without the
> water, one long, strong cord, to hold the same bear fishing or
> washing himself in the river Thames. The King at Windsor.

Along with the animal's new fishing outfit the sheriffs paid for a
thick wrap for his devoted keeper, who was expected to accom-

---

* At least I have been told by London Zoo that their 1829 bear was 'almost certainly' called Samson. How do they know? 'Because *all* the early polar bears were
called Samson.' Regrettably, my researches have failed to turn up any 'Samson'
polar bears in captivity today.
† Making twopence.

pany him into the Thames on his fishing expeditions (quite why remains a mystery); on less energetic days the bear could always fish from his place on the bank, doubtless to the relief of his put-upon companion. Hard as this may be to imagine nowadays, this was a time when the Thames was clean enough to have copious salmon in it – even three centuries later, in 1577, the chronicler Raphael Holinshed recorded that 'the water ittself is very cleare' and that 'fat and sweet salmons [are] dailie taken.' The king's new pet must have been delighted at the daily fare.

Foreign visitors coming to London for diplomacy or trade in the mid–thirteenth century, approaching by boat as most did, would have seen an extraordinary spectacle as they reached the Pool of London: in the middle distance the huge spire of old St Paul's Cathedral;* ahead of them, just upstream, the new massive stone London Bridge, the only river crossing in the city, with noisy, crowded Borough fruit and vegetable market spreading on to its southern end from the Southwark bank; and to their right the walls of the great Tower with – on the north bank just yards away – a large polar bear sitting lazily in the sun, casually pawing salmon out of the water . . .

No sooner had London become used to this oddity that had settled so comfortably among them than a yet more wonderful and strange creature appeared, landing at Michaelmas, 1255, at 'Wythsand' (probably Sandwich) on the Kent coast. Led by

---

* The spire of St Paul's at this time reached an amazing 489 feet above ground; at that height, had it survived with its spire intact, it would still have been one of the tallest buildings in the world at the outbreak of World War I.

his keeper, Henricus de Flor, the animal walked the long Canterbury–London road towards the capital, and finally entered the city by boat up the Thames, with crowds – marveling and perhaps somewhat alarmed – gathering by the roadside and riverside as he made his grand entrance.

This gift from another in-law of Henry's, the French king Louis IX (who had, as most French kings did in such times, much to be conciliatory about), was brought back as a trophy from his crusades in Palestine. The arrival of this beast was considered such a momentous event that the now ageing chronicler Matthew Paris (monk and historian) left his abbey at St Albans to journey down to London to see the marvel with his own eyes. He described what he saw: 'The beast is about ten years old, possessing a rough hide rather than fur, has small eyes at the top of its head, and eats and drinks with a trunk.'

And in his *Chronica Majora*, with great consideration for those unable to witness this strange sight firsthand (and for the benefit of posterity too), he even supplied two pictures, one of them showing the animal's keeper, 'that one might better understand the size thereof.' Unsurprisingly Paris's drawings of this African elephant are incomparably more realistic than an earlier elephant picture he completed in 1248, or any of the camel drawings he used to illustrate his maps of the Holy Land, none of which he had had the opportunity to make from life.*

Besides Matthew Paris's drawings, there is one surviving image

---

* Besides his elephants, the most natural-looking animal drawings he carried out were of sea monsters. At least, they *seem* natural-looking.

of Henry's elephant, and in the strangest place. If you walk into the Cathedral Church of St Peter in Exeter, and walk around to the south quire aisle behind the bishop's throne, you'll find the old misericords (folding seats) on display. There is a carving on the back of one of these depicting an elephant. It is surprisingly naturalistic (in spite – it must be said – of having very peculiar ears), and if not done from the life (which seems unlikely) was at least done from a firsthand drawing. Its date suggests that this may well be the very same elephant sent by Louis, Henry's new beast just lately arrived in the Tower.

It is almost impossible to imagine the extraordinary experience of seeing an elephant for the first time; those of us brought up with accessible public zoos, *National Geographic* and the Discovery

Matthew Paris's drawing of Henry III's new elephant and his keeper, from Paris's Chronica Majora.

The carving of an elephant on a misericord in Exeter Cathedral.

Channel have always known what these things look like, but it was not always thus. Stories featuring elephants would have been well known to most Londoners – Hannibal crossing the Alps perhaps best known of all – but the sight of a living, moving elephant, seen up close and walking the city streets, weary and melancholy, must have been overwhelming. Yes, people would have seen pictures and heard stories, but they would have been equally familiar with pictures and stories of unicorns, mermaids, Cyclopses, sirens, flying horses and talking pigs; such creatures featured regularly in bestiaries (illustrated books of beasts) of the period, described and illustrated with neither more nor less scepticism than snakes, giraffes, crocodiles, lions, elephants or eagles. No categorical distinction was made, nor would it be for many centuries yet. Even in the sixteenth century, when the chronicler John Stow came to record the arrival of Frederick's leopards in his *Annals of London* ('The Emperour sent to K. Henry three leopards, in token of his regall shield of Armes,' etc.), the report is preceded by another item of similar zoological interest: 'In the moneth of June in the South part of England by the Sea coast were seene two great Dragons in the ayre, flying and fighting together a whole day, the one chasing the other to the deepe sea, and then were no more seene.'[*] (So maybe after excitement like this the average thirteenth-century Londoner would have found a plodding, earthbound elephant terribly dull.)

The sheriffs of London were now called upon to build (and, more to the point, to pay a sum in excess of £22 for) a great wooden elephant house. Although they had only lately managed – at some expense – to make viable living arrangements for the nuisance polar bear, they were keen not to upset His Majesty the King by refusing the latest request, having just been imprisoned (albeit briefly) following the escape of a prisoner from Newgate. So they did not hesitate to obey orders with commendable alacrity and good grace. It was further made clear that the house should be built 'in such a fashion and of such strength as to be fit for other uses when required' – the implication being that it might one day become necessary to house human prisoners there instead.

---

[*] This does of course beg a question – assuming for a moment that the dragon account is less than completely accurate, why should we trust such a source? The prosaic reason is that on many subjects Stow is all we have, and as far as we can tell he is *usually* reliable.

Displaying a burst of apparent animal-loving almost worthy of the modern age, the king had decreed that his elephant should not be meanly crammed into tiny lodgings, but should have a spacious house, measuring 20 feet by 40; this magnanimous gesture gave the elephant a room approximately half the size of a doubles tennis court.[*] Such comfort for an animal, even a royal animal, was unprecedented.[†]

It is no wonder that the royal elephant was popular with the public. But in spite of all the attention, the elephant's keepers apparently had not yet quite mastered the art of taking care of this 'beast most strange and wonderful to the English people,' and his living conditions proved – to everyone's surprise at the time, if not so now – to be less than adequate.

So much so that, sure enough, the animal was dead before two years were up. In 1257 he was buried in the Tower grounds, probably close to the Chapel of St Peter ad Vincula, where the headless body of Anne Boleyn was to be buried three centuries later. He did not rest in peace, however, for in August 1258 his bones were dug up and sent by the constable of the Tower to William Taylard, sacrist of Westminster. It seems that the first ele-

---

[*] Far larger than the average London family house of the day, incidentally.

[†] And in fact it's not too bad even by modern standards. As a point of comparison: when the last elephants were moved from London Zoo in 2001, the indoor part of their enclosure measured 33 feet x 33; in other words almost exactly the same as the 1255 house – but the one built in 1967 was housing not one but three animals. The 2001 move took the lucky trio to a site at Whipsnade covering about six acres, which no doubt would have impressed even the devoted Frederick.

phant to walk the English streets still had a part to play in the country's spiritual life — if you visit the Reliquary Room of the Victoria & Albert Museum today, you will see a number of thirteenth-century reliquaries and caskets, made of bone and ivory. (Of course, Taylard's intentions may have been less scrupulous; you'll be amazed how many Genuine Relics of the Saints you can get out of one decent-sized elephant skeleton.)

Throughout their often short lives all these Tower animals remained in the care of the 'Keeper of His Majesty's Lions and Leopards' (later retitled 'Master of the King's Bears and Apes,' as the collection began to diversify), who was still (as far as we know) the surprisingly resilient William de Botton. He had been appointed to the post soon after the arrival in the Tower of the first leopards, and from then had had full responsibility for the feeding of all the animals, maintaining their living quarters and so on.

The increase in de Botton's workload since the early days must have been significant too; for by 1255 he had responsibility for the welfare not only of the old lion (whose provenance remains unknown), Louis IX's elephant (beginning his tragically short sojourn in his large wooden elephant house) and the Norwegian polar bear (still fishing happily on the bank of the Thames), but also all the many and various Woodstock beasts, each requiring (at least, requiring in an ideal world) different living conditions, diets, patterns of exercise and so on. (Frederick's leopards, you will recall, did not make it nearly this far.) And the poor man wasn't as young as he used to be.

We know next to nothing about William de Botton. The time would eventually come when his odd post would be given as an

honor to a member of the nobility,* just as the positions of lieutenant and constable of the Tower were to become, centuries
later, fairly symbolic but much-coveted positions, given as a reward
to one who had done the country – or, more often, the monarch –
good service (like Richard III's lieutenant, Robert Brackenbury, or
George IV's constable, the Duke of Wellington – of whom more
later), so the keeper of the animals in the Tower Menagerie
became if not exactly an enviable position, then at least in theory
primarily a position of privilege. But in the early years it seems that
the incumbents were minor household officials, and as such would
almost certainly have been expected to do much of the dirty work
themselves (later, noble incumbents would have had minions to do
the less desirable parts of the job, I have no doubt).

It was not until the nineteenth century, a full six hundred years
after the establishment of the Menagerie, that an appointment to
the keepership was made on the basis of the candidate's proven
experience of working with animals; and the first qualified keeper
was also the last, for ironically it was that keeper, Alfred Cops,
who ended up overseeing the Menagerie's demise.

Besides the feeding and keeping of the collection, another major
responsibility fell into de Botton's large and varied portfolio, the
enabling and organizing of public access to the animals, for select

---

* As with many leading members of the Royal Household, even to the present day,
who are not the usual class of domestic servant. Unusually for such a position,
however, it came with a reasonable (and not symbolic) salary attached – but primarily the position would have been accepted for the honor, not for the
honorarium (nor presumably for the job satisfaction).

members of The Public would soon be allowed into the Tower grounds to gawk at them in all their strangeness – providing some extra revenue for keeper if not for Crown. The Menagerie was not yet, as it was later to become, a hugely popular tourist attraction, drawing hundreds of visitors daily, but as the collection grew and changed it did attract a certain amount of interest. Although there had been lions, hyenas, camels and the like in the country for some time, at Woodstock and in other smaller private collections, never before had a wider public (rather than just royalty, nobility and their friends) had direct access to such sights themselves. The attraction had been all the greater since the arrival at the Tower of the remains of the old family collection from Oxfordshire. The turnover of visitors may not have been great, but with the Woodstock animals on public view too, we cannot underestimate the impact this impressive collection must have had. God, it would seem, was truly capable of creating wonders.

Although the Tower itself was soon to become the center of a power struggle between King Henry and his newly appointed justiciar, Hugh Bigod, the king's animal collection continued to thrive there apparently undisturbed. But for all the documentation we have regarding the day-to-day workings of the Menagerie during this period, there remain significant and surprising gaps in our knowledge. There was little use for 'writing-down,' except when absolutely necessary for official matters, mainly accounts and the like. And as all writing (with the exception of the odd chronicle) had its prescribed official function, there is nothing descriptive, nothing random or frivolous or characterful, except by accident. What we know about the Menagerie in this period must then be gleaned imaginatively from such records.

To do the recorders and the chroniclers justice, it should be emphasized that we do in fact know quite a considerable amount, an extraordinary amount given the length of time that has since passed: we know what the collection contained (from a few observers keen to record sightings of rarities in chronicles, official documents and account books), and there are fairly complete records of how much things cost, how much was budgeted to support the lions, leopards, elephants and keepers, what the animals ate and so on.

But there is also a great deal of information that has not survived, or perhaps was never even recorded. Most surprising is the fact that to our misfortune nobody knows where in the extensive Tower grounds the Menagerie actually was in these years, where exactly all these animals were kept, fed, visited and ultimately in many cases swiftly buried.

We can assume that apart from the Norwegian polar bear (who was given special treatment for reasons of economy) the animals would certainly have been kept within the Tower grounds, that is, somewhere within the curtain wall. Henry had intimated that the elephant house would find other uses when vacant, and when the time came a couple of decades later it was indeed reused, this time to house rebellious humans.[*] Keeping

---

[*] The volume of human prisoners in the Tower may well have increased after 1257 when the duties of the constable of the Tower had expanded to include overall jurisdiction over the city; and when in the early years of the reign of Edward I many hundreds of Jews were imprisoned in the Tower (following a typical reversal of fortune – a generation earlier it had been the place where their community had taken refuge), at least some of the overflow from the main cells was indeed kept in the elephant house.

one's dangerous prisoners just *outside* one of the strongest fortresses in Europe would hardly have been sensible practice. But from the fact that certain members of the public had frequent (though limited) access to the enclosures we can conclude that they would have been somewhere in the outer bailey, that is, not within the inner fortress walls. It would hardly have been appropriate to allow the common people – unreliable and seditious as they were prone to be in such politically shaky times – to wander freely around the central grounds; after all, this was still a royal residence, albeit one that was used as such very infrequently. It is not impossible to guess where the elephant house might have stood, if only because its proportions limit the possibilities, given what we know about the other buildings and walls standing at the time.

But there is no reason to assume that at this early stage the animals were necessarily kept close together. There is something slightly ad hoc about all the arrangements relating to the animals, and the idea of odd animals and animal houses scattered about, crammed into any corner that would fit them, is pleasingly in keeping with this general impression.

The polar bear's house, we can guess, would have been reasonably close to the riverside (to make the nerve-racking process of walking him to catch his lunch a little easier). At the beginning of the next century there is a reference to a gate 'between the King's Chamber [then in the Lanthorn Tower] and the *berehous*'; if this was built for the first bear in the Tower, our Norwegian polar bear, it would have put him in the inner ward, towards the eastern side, right beside Henry's private rooms; and as the king was so rarely there this would hardly have been seen as much of a problem.

That the king lived at the Tower only very rarely may have had something to do with the state of the place at that difficult time. Especially between about 1258 (the year of Bigod's appointment as justiciar) and 1262, the bitter power struggle being acted out in the Tower caused utter chaos in that dense little site on the bank of the Thames. Yet it was there that the king chose to take refuge with his wife and his young son Edward, when things became really bad. Before long Henry would learn that the nobleman Simon de Montfort, the controversial crusader for reform, was capable of causing far more trouble than Bigod ever did, and the country found its allegiances sharply divided. In the midst of the troubles, the heir to the throne would earn the nickname 'Leopard Prince.' The *Song of Lewes* (a long political poem written in Latin around 1264, with a strong anti-Henry, pro–de Montfort agenda) explained: 'Perhaps he will rightly be called a Leopard . . . Leo: brave, proud and fierce . . . and the pard: wily, devious and treacherous.'

Henry's long and troubled reign came to an end on 16 November 1272. The Leopard Prince, now Edward I, was to prove himself a stronger and less troubled king than his father had been. Edward was a natural soldier and gifted lawmaker and administrator. He soon took significant steps to improve the Tower, making it both a safer and more comfortable place for himself and his queens to spend the occasional day, and – more importantly – a stronger fortress. The new outer wall and moat that Edward created resulted in the need for a new entranceway from the land side; and so were constructed the western gate and barbican that became known, respectively, as the Lion Gate and the Lion Tower.[*]

The drawbridge at the new Lion Gate soon became the only way into the Tower complex; crossing this drawbridge then took you into the new barbican where we assume (because the name 'Lion Tower' was adopted very early and stuck at once) the royal animals were soon being housed. All visitors to the Tower would have had to pass through the animal yard, then, on their way through the old Middle Tower towards the center of the complex. Perhaps the more unwelcome visitors were meant to be intimidated by this, to think twice before trying to force their way into the building – these animals, even caged, would have been imposing and frightening, and could not but have given pause to even the most strong-hearted.[†] Even at night, approaching in darkness, it would have been possible to hear the animals and smell them all too keenly. Visitors to the Tower today use an entrance on an almost identical site, and beside

---

[*] The first reference to this building by the name 'the Lion Turret' appears in 1338. It may be that this artificial island on the entrance causeway was constructed for some other purpose, probably to house the Exchange; but sometime after 1285 the king had the Exchange moved out, and his animals moved in. John Stow wrote that the beasts had been housed in the western barbican since the days of Edward I, and in this instance we have no reason to doubt him.

[†] I imagine this worked rather like a 'Beware of the Dog' sign. Even if you can see that the dog is on a chain, the frantic barking and straining on the chain should be enough of a deterrent to the uninvited. One might hope that an agitated lion would be even more effective. 'Beware ye Lyones.'

the open ruins of the Lion Tower's drawbridge pit the Middle Tower still stands, the first stop for every conscientious tourist.*

After a highly unconvincing start, the Menagerie now had a semi-purpose-built home, and under the Leopard Prince it found itself settling onto a site it was to occupy for the best part of six centuries.

---

* Early in 1999 the Lion Tower was excavated by the Oxford Archaeological Unit as part of a major Historic Royal Palaces project. The dig, which took just four days, was the first archaeological excavation of a zoo in Britain. To limit disruption to visitors, excavation was limited to a single trench, measuring just 19 feet x 13 feet. Besides the ubiquitous clay pipes and bits of miscellaneous pottery, the team found several fragments of animal bone. None of these belonged to the wild beasts housed there (their bodies would not have been simply left to rot in their cages, obviously), but to cattle, sheep, domestic fowl and dogs, the relics of many a carnivorous lunch several centuries ago. Some of the bones show 'evidence of some butchery,' says the report; others, more vivid still, of 'gnaw damage.'

2

Fearful Symmetry

For every virtue and for every sin there is an example drawn from bestiaries, and animals exemplify the human world.

—Umberto Eco, *The Name of the Rose*

At the close of the reign of Henry III, the experience of seeing an animal not native to southern England would have been the privilege of only a tiny minority of the London population. Admittedly there were rather more things running wild in England then than now, with animals such as wolves still roaming freely over much of the country; but for most people other than those few who by chance had managed to glimpse a more exotic royal-owned animal on its way to Woodstock or the Tower (Henry's leopards, polar bear or elephant, for example) all such creatures remained firmly restricted to the national imagination.

More often than not their imagination was wildly inaccurate, of course, with (we now know) the most fanciful ideas about how these animals looked and acted. For most people the most authoritative notion of how an alien animal must look would have come from a bestiary, an illustrated book of beasts originating in the classical *Physiologus* (produced by Aristotle, among others); these didactic books listed and described a huge range of the kinds of creatures one would be hard pressed to find wandering through Cheapside market of an afternoon – elephants, lions, crocodiles, hyenas and, still more glamorously to our eyes, dragons, griffins, unicorns and so on. Uniquely popular in this period, these books would feature a few dozen animals, each represented by an image and a few lines' description. The prime function of a bestiary, however, was not to inform or educate people about natural history; rather the animals were used by the creators of bestiaries to explore and promote their allegorical and symbolic values (so any resemblance to actual living things was purely coincidental). Vultures were believed to be omens of human death and so were often portrayed with corpses, hyenas (nasty and untrustworthy) were depicted as grave-robbers, and so on. The more the animal's characteristic features could be captured in the illustrations, the more useful the book would be in educating a largely illiterate public.

So bestiaries were no great help in distinguishing creatures that do exist from those we now assume to be imaginary, or their real characteristics from their fabulous ones. This was largely because when a French, Italian or English illuminator wanted to produce a bestiary, his information had to come from somewhere, and the somewhere was always, always questionable. The illuminator had no lions, eagles or dragons to examine, to describe and draw from the life, so had to make do with what he had – mythological tales, lore and pictures from older bestiaries. As a result,

Animals from the Queen Mary Psalter, an equal mix of the real and the imaginary, jumbled together with no sense at all that this might be a little odd.

mistakes and misunderstandings were rarely corrected and frequently compounded and exaggerated. Pictures of serpents with legs or ostriches with short necks and cloven hoofs were common. Equally unsurprising, given the total absence of any sources of information to contradict these pictures, the mistakes and misapprehensions that appeared in bestiaries gained a public currency that they retained for centuries. The popular belief in elephants' inordinate longevity (a propensity to live many, many centuries, we are told) and natural timidity (a terror of mice in particular) were among the most enduring. Another longstanding favorite was the notion that lion cubs were born dead, and that they had their life breathed into them by the parent-lion – very Christian (and very Narnia too, for that matter).

In some cases it was many centuries before these myths were exploded; though at least by the early seventeenth century Edward Topsell (in his *History of Four-Footed Beasts*), for example, was able to say, smugly, 'It hath been falsely supposed that all Tigers be female and that they engender in copulation with the wind.' At least they'd cleared that one up by then. On the other hand Topsell did have some trouble (misunderstandings, at the very least) with even the most banal, unexotic of animals, like cattle. Of 'Oxen,' he wrote:

There are Oxen in India will eat flesh like Wolves, and have but one horn, and whole hoofs; some also have three horns; there be other as high as Camels, and their horns four foot broad . . . In the Province of Bangala are Oxen which equall the Elephant in height.

And then there is its close relative, the 'Bucephalus,' which 'will eat anything either bread, broth, salted or powdered beef, grass or herbs, and the use hereof being alive is for hunting.'

With bestiary pictures that were more useful as dramatic story-telling aids than they were accurate depictions of the animals they were supposed to represent (likewise most other early depictions of animals, in illuminated manuscripts like the Luttrell Psalter), and with even the most responsible travel accounts full of wildly untrue mythology (more of these anon), it is hardly surprising that people – even those educated up to the point where they could and did read – could be persuaded of almost anything regarding the world outside their realm of experience. Ultimately the sources of bestiaries were the great writers of antiquity (Aristotle, Pliny), and these were held in the highest possible reverence.

Once Londoners and their guests were finally able to see some of these wonders in the Tower, it became possible at least in part to identify what was and what was not true about them, distinguishing between the real and the fantastic; yet it would not be long before these animals would begin to spawn new superstitions of their own. The elephant who could only drink wine, the ostriches who could digest iron, the lions who could predict the weather, or the death of the monarch, or could tell whether or not a woman was a virgin – all these creatures in their time would come to the Tower Menagerie, and all would be accepted unquestioned.

Traveling with his queen in Gascony in 1288, Henry III's son King Edward I showed his support of the Menagerie by sending back to the Tower a lion and a lynx (an 'ounce') he had acquired. And with them he sent four men to care for them (Jacobus Petri and his three sons) to whom he allocated wages of 3*d* each per day, on top of the 10*d* a day set aside for the keep of their charges. Unsurprisingly the Tower's own in-house 'Keeper of the King's Lions and Leopards' was far better remunerated by now. Around this time the deal was improved still further to include a prime lodging in the Tower grounds. It may not have been an easy job, but at least the money and the perks were good; and conditions weren't bad – at least, not for the staff.

The king's young son Edward may have watched these animals' arrival in England when he and his sister traveled down to Dover to meet their parents on their return from Gascony. The lion and lynx had been in the Tower about a year when the young prince paid them his first visit in their new home. A boy of just five, the heir to the throne was being brought up outside the capital, at Langley in Hertfordshire (where his father kept a camel for his entertainment), but often spent his summers traveling in and around London. The Tower the young Edward saw that year had only lately undergone substantial work. His father had invested even more than Henry III, in a new moat and a second curtain wall outside his fortress, this time surrounding all four sides of the complex, including the waterfront, thus landlocking it completely. This pair of concentric walls made the Tower far and away the strongest fortress in Europe.

Much of this work was paid for with profits from the Mint in the western part of the Tower grounds; making money at this time was an extremely lucrative business, turning a profit of at least 9*d* per pound of silver, after expenses. The refortified Tower, in the custody of John de Burgh (granted by the king as part of a quiet little territorial deal), now also boasted a fully rebuilt chapel (St Peter ad Vincula) and new royal lodgings at the top of St Thomas's Tower. As part of the rearrangement, significant new powers were granted to the constable of the Tower, among them the ability to hear court cases in the king's absence.

By the time the young prince made his first recorded visit to the Tower animals, he would have been treated not only to the sight of the lion and lynx, but also to another 'white bear.' This is unlikely to have been his grandfather Henry's Norwegian bear of 1252 (for one thing such a lifespan would be quite considerable for a polar bear in captivity, even today). Besides the references to payment for the keeper ('Iohanni de Navesby custodi urse albe in Turri Londinie') another payment had been made a couple of years earlier, on 13 April 1287, dealing with the transport of a white bear from a place called Lynn to the Tower by sea (up the Thames, in other words). Assuming that this wasn't the old bear who had been taken to the seaside for his recreation (and I think it's a reasonable assumption), it seems that a replacement had been sought for that original bear, probably now dead, who had fished for his food from the bank of the Thames a long reign ago.

Within a couple of years a leopard had been added to the set the young prince had seen; it had been brought back for the king by the ambassadors he had sent off on a mission to Central Asia; their diplomatic efforts with the Mongol Khan had not been as successful as Edward would have liked, but at least they brought him the leopard (exciting in itself), and at the same time – with great optimism – introduced the parasol to England.

In 1307, at the age of twenty-three, Edward Prince of Wales became Edward II, and so began another deeply troubled and divisive reign, which inspired Marlowe's tragedy *Edward II* (and Derek Jarman's disturbing and imaginative film adaptation), and perhaps is remembered mainly for tales of Edward's brutal murder at Berkeley Castle twenty years after his accession to the throne. With a temperament little suited to the job required of him, Edward did not try to hide his preference for rural pursuits over court life (he was, by all accounts, something of a master at thatching, hedging and gardening), for music over warfare and politics (Marlowe wrote that 'Music and poetry is his delight'), and for Piers Gaveston and Hugh le Despenser over his own long-suffering wife, Isabella (long-suffering but, it must be said, politically a great deal more astute than her husband). According to Marlowe, at least, it would seem that Edward's reign was doomed even before it began.

Faced with the real threat of a civil war, one of Edward's first acts as monarch was to order new fortifications to be built for the Tower, and the replacement of its constable. When times were bad it would be the Tower that would have to serve as his refuge, and it would have to be absolutely loyal and strong enough to withstand even the most aggressive of attacks. Later in his reign the threat of an invasion by the king of France, allied to Edward's own queen, led him to fortify the Tower's river wall. But, as his great-grandson Richard II was to find out, mere fortifications wouldn't be enough to keep a determined people out of the Tower, and as it happened this turned out to be the least of Edward's worries.

Yet with the momentum of a century's history behind it, the Menagerie carried on regardless. Edward found the time, reluctantly as we might guess, to arrange for the animals to be fed, and fed well; from 1314 the City, ever bountiful, supplied the king's lion with a quarter of mutton (quite literally a quarter of a sheep) every day.* A later writ ensured that 6d was allotted for each large animal (lion or leopard) every day (at a time when human prisoners were allowed only a penny daily), again out of the purse of the City. And the keepers of each animal received 3 sous (three halfpence) daily, regularly and promptly.

Well, perhaps 'promptly' isn't quite accurate – at one point in 1318, when Edward had been on the throne for a decade and all around him had begun to crumble (Gaveston had been executed and Edward was effectively a puppet of Lancaster and his council), the unfortunate keeper was owed £9 7s 6d, a considerable sum (close to $7,350 today), and about a year's wages. And there was little he could do in protest; weak and unpopular Edward may have been, but it would still have been quite impossible for any employee who valued his livelihood (after all, the keepers did in relative terms make a very good living) to complain and survive with position and salary (and neck) intact. When a similar problem was faced by William Bounde, one of Henry IV's keepers, in 1408, he lodged an official complaint (claiming that his creditors would have him put in debtors' prison and the royal animals would surely starve in his absence), and was in fact paid the £55 due to him quite promptly. But almost as promptly he found himself unemployed and slinking back to the family home . . .

In these days the keepership was still given to a member of the

---

* One can't help being dismayed to think how many starving London families this might have fed then.

king's household. Through the first two centuries of its existence it was given to several 'yeomen of the king's chamber,' a
'yeoman of the king's armour within the Tower,' an 'usher of the
king's chamber,' a 'porter of the king's wardrobe' and so on. All
probably saw it as a promotion of sorts. It was granted for life,
usually, though on certain occasions it would appear that a pro-
bationary period was served out first, usually a year or so. Most
were allowed to die on the job; William Bounde, the one who
had complained about nonpayment of his wages, was one of
only a handful who didn't. On the whole the records refer to
appointments 'in the same manner as [the previous keeper],
deceased.'

To begin with, the keepership was not given as an acknowledged title, merely a responsibility – as far as we can see nobody
was given a title of 'Keeper of the King's Lions' (or similar) in the
earliest years, but grants were made to pay them for the particular responsibility, appointing them to 'the custody of' or 'the
keeping of' the animals. The wages for the post were fixed early,
and remained constant – each new appointment makes reference
simply to 'the usual wages.' For Robert le Bowyer, of Doncaster,
this had been defined as sixpence a day for his wages, and 'for the
sustenance of each lion, lioness and leopard 6d. and of each whelp
4d.' This rate remained unchanged for over a century.

All these appointments appear in the Patent Rolls, the public
records (so called because the pages were sewn into long, con-
tinuous rolls) that have recorded royal grants since the beginning
of the thirteenth century. The entry for 5 August 1349, for
instance, gives us all the information we need in a typical formula:

Marlborough. Grant, for life, to John Styrop of the keeping of the king's lions in the Tower of London, in the same manner as Robert de Doncastre, deceased, held it of the king's grant, with the usual wages.

Mandate in pursuance to John Darcy, keeper of the said Tower, or his lieutenant.

Besides these there were still the payments being made to keepers of particular animals (probably those who did both the dangerous work and the dirty work). When Edward III's son, the Black Prince, sent a lion back from Gascony around 1360, for example, he would also have sent a keeper back with him, to accompany him on the journey and look after him in his new home.

The Tower of London was a busy place. Its many functions meant that there was always a considerable amount of coming and going in the riverside site. The Royal Wardrobe, costly and impressive, did travel around the country, but until 1361 had its base here at the Tower. The Royal Mint had been in place here since 1300, and here it would remain until the start of the nineteenth century when limitations of space dictated that (as in the case of the Menagerie) a new home would have to be found for it. And of course the Tower remained a royal residence throughout. It was here that the queen lived in 1321, while her husband was away at war with the recalcitrant Welsh, and here that she gave birth to their daughter, Princess Joanna.

One of the most remarkable events to take place in the Tower this century was the climax of the rather misnamed Peasants'

Revolt (a major uprising led by a group of people who were distinctly nonpeasants). In June 1381 a group of them marched on the capital. The beleaguered Richard was forced to leave his chambers in the Tower (his quarters there were only yards from where he was later to keep his private camel, a gift from the people of London in 1392, when relations were rather better.)[*] During his brief absence the fortress was stormed, and breached, and ransacked; none of the drawbridges, portcullises or moats was able to keep the revolters out, and apparently the roaring lions did not do a great deal to put them off either. Richard was forced to capitulate (though only temporarily). Londoners quarreled frequently with Richard; by Christmas 1387 he would again be forced into submission at their hands, cowering in the Tower in fear of his life.[†]

It is not inappropriate, then, that perhaps most famously of all its functions the Tower still served as a prison; at times it housed large numbers of inmates (a massive 600 Jews in 1278 − 293 were later hanged), though usually a few but of the highest quality (residents in the summer of 1305, for instance, included William Wallace, known as 'Braveheart,' who had fought to free Scotland from King Edward's oppressive yoke). And it was a truly vile place to be kept. Torture of prisoners was not unusual, and the heads of executed traitors – Welsh princes and the like – were prominently displayed

---

[*] On the same occasion the queen was given a pelican, probably representing 'piety.' I cannot begin to speculate as to the symbolism of the camel.

[†] It will have come as a surprise to no one that when the time came to make their choice the support of the capital would fall behind Henry Bolingbroke, a decision that would put the last nail in Richard's coffin.

on spikes on the ramparts. In the reign of Edward I a senior official called Henry de Bray, faced with the prospect of imprisonment in the Tower, in sheer terror tried to drown himself on the boat ride there, throwing himself (bound) into the Thames; failing in this, he then, once inside the Tower, tried to dash his skull against a wall, but was equally unsuccessful. He did eventually succeed in committing suicide in his cell not long afterwards.

Four centuries later Horace Walpole was to write (tongue definitely in cheek) that the Tower would perhaps not be such a bad place to be imprisoned, for all the interesting things one would have to see there – 'There are a thousand pretty things there to amuse you: the lions, the Armoury, the Crown, King Henry's codpiece, and the axe that beheaded Anne Boleyn.' But the truth was that most prisoners at the Tower would have been kept far from sight of the animal collection (if only because by this time it was probably situated on the Tower's main entrance-exit causeway). In the whole history of the Menagerie I am aware of just one reference to a prisoner being allowed to see the king's collection, when the French king John II was residing there having been captured by Edward III in the Battle of Poitiers (Edward's son the Black Prince was also in France around this time, and this was probably when he sent the lion and keeper home from Gascony). John's expense books covering his detention at the Tower include an entry for Tuesday, 2 June 1360: 'Tuesday June second. The keeper of the lions of the King of England. A gift given him by the King for showing him the lions; three nobles, worth 20s.' Even in prison, in other words, King John was sufficiently self-possessed and gracious not to forget to give the animals' keeper a generous tip.

In every way the Tower's other functions made it an awkward place to keep animals, and an utterly ludicrous place to try to run a zoo that was to be opened to the public. Managing the flow of paying visitors became a new task falling under the remit of the animals' keepers, as it would not be long before the Tower would open its doors to its first tourists.

Access would have been limited, of course, and restricted to a small number of carefully selected people (those with the right friends, perhaps). But for those happy few, the experience of seeing these creatures live for the first time must have given them a real thrill. They had seen them before in books, of course, but this was quite something else.

Now, *pictures* of animals were everywhere, and long had been. Bestiaries had not been the only place where pictorial representations of animals could be found, of course – far from it. Even setting aside books of hours (illustrated devotional books) and psalters and the like, medieval art is littered with paintings of Noah's Ark or the Garden of Eden, dense with fauna; with St Jeromes and lions, St Georges and dragons, with unicorns on royal crests and tapestries.

A distinction must be drawn here between depictions of animals that do make a claim to accuracy – books of zoology and their ilk – and those whose apparent function is something quite different. The difference between Rubens's lion (which looks like a lion) and Dürer's various lions (which sometimes look more like Lassie than anything you'll see claiming to be a lion in *National Geographic*) is not *alone* attributable to the resources the artist had at his disposal – simply put, to whether real-life models meant that accuracy/naturalism was an option at all – but also to the artist's style and intentions. This question of function is paramount – the animals Leonardo da Vinci drew in long-studied detail at the local court menagerie were not drawn primarily for symbolic reasons, and the St Jerome lions were (Dürer did several pictures of St Jerome with his trademark lion). The fact that St Jerome pictures seldom feature lions that look like lions has nothing to do with the artist's skill and everything to do with the function of the art and the animal's place in it.

Compare Dürer's St Jerome lions with his famous rhinoceros, for example, that amazing image of Pope Leo X's new pet that Dürer produced from descriptions and other likenesses of the animal. This picture was intended simply to record, and it is extraordinary – indeed, it was his woodcut that made the animal famous across Europe. His lions were quite a different matter, ranging from naturalistic drawings (at least one carried out from the life, when he visited a menagerie in Ghent) to the strangely human-looking lions in certain of the Jeromes.*

The function of an art that privileges naturalism, that takes its value precisely from being drawn from the life, is altogether different from this kind of emblematic, richly symbolic art, just as it is different in intention from other forms, such as fabulous illustrations of travel narratives. Like Matthew Paris's uniquely early life-drawings of Henry III's elephant, of 1254, or his contempo-

---

* Needless to say, even those pictures that make claims to accuracy (unlike Jerome lions) cannot always be trusted. Take the example of illustrations to slightly fabulous travelers' tales; or Johann Johnston's 1653 book *Historiae Naturalis de Serpentibus et Draconibus*, in which he produces detailed drawings of several different species of dragon (see p. 55).

Dürer's drawing of two lions, c. 1520, and famous engraving of a rhinoceros, 1515.

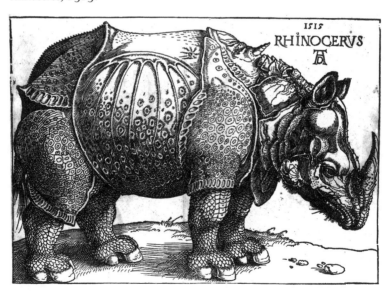

rary Villard de Honnecourt's from-the-life animal pictures on the continent, illustrations may be meant not to excite wonder but to record. Dramatic pictures of St George fighting a snarling dragon have an entirely different agenda, and call on entirely different skills in both artist and viewer.

George Eliot considered these differences, in *Adam Bede*. She writes:

> The pencil is conscious of a delightful facility in drawing a griffin – the longer the claws, and the larger the wings, the better; but that marvellous facility which we mistook for genius, is apt to forsake us when we want to draw a real unexaggerated lion.

So even should you want to disentangle the imaginary or enchanted from the real, the 'truthful' and the mundane (however impressive), it is not an easy thing to do. This applies, she continues, to the distinction between writing 'truth' and writing exaggerated 'falsehood': 'Examine your words well, and you will find that even when you have no motive to be false, it is a very hard thing to say the exact truth.'

So after centuries of drawing from the imagination, from written descriptions or from other illustrations *faute de mieux* – even the best artists may find that (even faced with a real living model – a caged lion, say) old habits die hard.

Besides, it would be a silly exaggeration to say that the Menagerie brought instant realism to the depiction of animals, but it did make a degree of realism at least a possibility. Too many artistic (stylistic or symbolic) factors determine the way in which an animal is portrayed by any artist at any time in any particular picture, especially in religious art where symbolic or iconographic significance is of supreme importance, but it was for the first time *possible* to draw from the life, not from stylized bestiary imagery. There the animals were, living, before your very eyes, should you but choose to use them.

However, the fact that the fifteenth century saw the beginning of a new possibility of artistic portrayals of animals from the life is somewhat academic. In practice the combination of sixteenth-century Protestantism (which didn't approve of images) and seventeenth-century Puritanism (which didn't approve of anything much) was soon to lead to an almost total stunting of visual art in Britain. The only survivor was the art of portraiture, but with few exceptions (the expert miniaturist Nicholas Hilliard predominant among these) all of Britain's best portrait artists in the seventeenth century were really Dutch or German.

So after the Middle Ages, with its books of hours, its bestiaries and the like, Britain effectively experienced a three-hundred-year drought, with few paintings, naturalistic or otherwise, and fewer still – if indeed any – of exotic animals, real or imaginary. While Titian was in Venice, putting the finishing touches on the beautiful pair of leopards in his *Bacchus and Ariadne*, Henry VIII was preparing the systematic dismantling of the icon-friendly Catholic Church, and singularly failing to encourage the development of English painting. This barren period only came to an end in the middle of the eighteenth century, which brought a swift and spectacular blossoming of British art. Portraitists, landscape painters, painters of grand historical and mythological scenes, with styles ranging from that of the morality-engraver William Hogarth, to

Five species of dragon, from Johann Johnston's Historiae Naturalis de Serpentibus et Draconibus.

that of the portraitist and painter of historical scenes Joshua Reynolds (first president of the Royal Academy), all spring into life in this period, among them (and not a moment too soon) a number of great portrayers of animals, including the most famous of these, the nature-painter George Stubbs (of whom more later).

Of course, great sculptors, carvers and architects emerged long before this, and the English Baroque predates Reynolds and Hogarth by a full century and more, but in painting there was nothing in early Renaissance England to rival the fervent outpouring of creativity that was already taking place across the Channel. All across Europe the visual arts were thriving, and pictures of animals were being incorporated into the work of all the great masters, often pictures based on sketches made at their local royal menagerie or seraglio. Much of what we know about the Italian menageries of the fifteenth century comes from the work of the painter and draughtsman Pisanello; but he was far from the only artist of the period to enrich his animal interests with live studies.

In Milan, for instance, Leonardo da Vinci, Renaissance man *par excellence*, would soon be painting monkeys from the court menagerie there and from his own private collection. He believed strongly that where possible an artist should use live models for his work: 'The painter's work will have little merit if he takes for his guide other pictures, but if he will learn from natural things he will bear good fruit.' In his notes towards a kind of treatise on painting, he explains how to study animals, to learn the workings of their anatomy, in order to be better able to capture their likenesses. With this study of live animals – and not just observation but often dissection too – Leonardo produced comparative anatomical drawings (the arms of humans and monkeys, for example, a page that Dürer was later to copy in his own notes) and was able to incorporate realistic-looking camels, bears, horses and other animals into his painting. (In 1515 he also designed a mechanical lion.)

Such rigorous study of anatomy, Leonardo wrote, will also help the artist to produce plausible-looking pictures of fantastic animals:

> You know that you cannot make any animal without it having its limbs such that each bears some resemblance to that of some one of the other animals. If therefore you wish to make one of your imaginary animals appear more natural – let us suppose it to be a dragon* – take for its head that of a mastiff or setter, for its eyes those of a cat, for its ears those of a porcupine, for its nose that of a greyhound, with the eyebrows of a lion, the temples of an old cock and the neck of a water-tortoise.

Rather more rigorous than George Eliot's view, then. This imaginative way of drawing imaginary creatures as if they were merely variations on real ones goes some way towards explaining the appearance of early portrayals of nonmythological animals. The less accessible ones were simply drawn as variations on the more accessible ones, which is why pre-Menagerie elephants often look

---

* It is surprising and much to Leonardo's credit that he is so absolutely certain dragons are imaginary.

Elephants, and other animals, as depicted in the late fourteenth century.

like long-nosed horses, crocodiles like miscolored, scaly wolves and so on.

Nonmythological animals such as lions had as well-defined and as significant symbolic and allegorical values assigned to them as unicorns and the like. And similarly it is worth remembering that although animals such as unicorns did have great symbolic value (symbolizing female chastity predominantly), this was not to say that people did not still believe that such things existed. In fact the opposite was most definitely true; largely I suspect because of their frequent appearances in the Bible, a belief in unicorns persisted more or less unchallenged until the fifteenth century. It is worth bearing this in mind when considering works of art like the *Dame à la Licorne*, the magnificent set of tapestries now displayed at the Cluny Museum of the Middle Ages in Paris, which are believed to have been completed around 1500 (see plate 5). The lion and the unicorn have equivalent symbolic values in these* – the power and justice of the former to the chastity of the latter, for example – so both are stylized, their expressions very human. Although the unicorn was known to be rarer than the lion, special in some way, there was no doubt that (like the lion) it did exist somewhere, and it might be possible to draw one from the life one day – who knows?

Questions about unicorns only really began to be asked in the sixteenth century, and doubts raised, but the stories didn't die as easily as those relating to other famous fabulous beasts. Indeed even in the eighteenth century the old theories of their scarcity (but existence, certainly) continued to be revived every time someone less than scrupulous got his hands on a narwhal tusk and wanted to make a little money.

The animal collection in the Tower continued to serve as a unique resource for the provision of artists' models throughout its lifetime of many centuries. This came to be most notably the case in the eighteenth century as English painting began to flourish, and great artists like George Stubbs and Edwin Landseer came to sketch the lions there, using these sketches towards some of their most beautiful work, their paintings and engravings, respectively. As Leonardo had recognized at the menagerie in Milan all those centuries earlier, the technical ability and discipline to achieve a certain level of naturalism, a close likeness, the

---

* Only in the relatively recent past did the tapestries acquire their current name, which for obvious reasons privileges the unicorn over the lion.

*'The Lion and the Porcupine' by Villard de Honnecourt
(thirteenth century).*

skill of good and well-observed draughtsmanship, was essential to any artist – however naturalistic the final work was intended to look, or not (hence Dürer's impeccable sketches of a lion from the life before departing stylistically from them to paint his Jerome lions). Such technique and skill were not merely an asset (allowing Stubbs to paint a rhino accurate enough to be of use to a man studying the animal's physiology, for instance), but an absolute requirement.

Some 535 years after Matthew Paris's from-the-life elephants, a young poet-artist (and by all accounts something of a madman) by the name of William Blake would have made his way downriver to the Tower from his Lambeth house to paint one of the two tigers then in residence there, the two tigers Goldsmith described as 'fierce and savage beyond measure.' Or perhaps I should say 'the two "Tygers"' ('burning bright, in the forest of the night'). And yes, admittedly everything about the beautiful picture is rather heightened (quite how heightened or silly depends on which of the first editions you look at), but it is still undoubtedly much more grounded, a much less wildly visionary image than other of Blake's works of the time.* For one thing it does look like a tiger, in a way that no bestiary animal ever did (see plate 6).

But back to King Richard. Richard did take some personal interest in the Tower, perhaps surprising given his own less than ideal

---

* Compare this, for instance, to its exact contemporary, the serpent on the title page of *Europe*, or the semimythologized swan in *America* with its extraordinary, preposterously long neck (not to mention the angelic figure riding it).

experiences there. Among other things he had new tiles put down in the Byward Tower, just east of the Menagerie – tiles depicting leopards, as it happens. The Menagerie itself continued, undisturbed by the political upheavals, by now well established in the western 'Lion Tower.' The man in charge of the upkeep of the Tower and several other royal buildings for part of Richard's reign (appointed in 1389) was Geoffrey Chaucer, son of a London merchant who some years earlier had had responsibility for all the city's customs and excise. Chaucer, who is now better known as the author of the *Canterbury Tales* (probably the most significant and influential work of literature of the century), only retained this position for two years; he was perhaps rather less gifted a clerk of the King's Works than a poet. And by the start of the new century both he and the king were dead.

Then follow the first kings of the House of Lancaster, the Henrys IV and V, father and son, whose reigns leave us fewer records and no anecdotal evidence relating to the Menagerie. What with the usurpation of the Crown and subsequent conscience-appeasing pilgrimages to the Holy Land (the father), and the Battle of Agincourt and subsequent treaty with France (the son), their reigns were hardly uneventful; but these events have no part to play in our story.

So I shall take a liberty and pass – confident and blasé – over these two reigns (pausing only briefly to note the damage wrought upon the city and the country by the Black Death, the plague that wiped out whole villages and decimated the population of London and the country), and will rejoin the happenings in and around the Lion Tower in 1422, at the start of Henry VI's long reign, just a dozen or so years before the great purge.

3
Travelers' Tales

[There were Gryphons on this island too, creatures which were] large enough and strong enough to carry off an elephant and drop it to the ground from such a height that it will break into pieces. When the elephant has landed, the Gryphon swoops down and feeds on its flesh.

—Sir John Mandeville, *Travels*

I know these things appear strange; but if the shadow of a doubt can remain in any person's mind, I say, let him take a voyage there himself, and there he will know I am a traveller of veracity.

—Baron Münchausen

By the time the infant Henry VI came to the throne the world had already begun to grow many-fold. Even in the short time since the young king's grandfather had taken the throne in 1399, Henry the Navigator of Portugal had begun his pioneering journeys of exploration around the west African coast. And the half-century that followed Henry VI's reign would see the horizon pushed further and still further, with Columbus's Caribbean discoveries, Vasco da Gama's rounding of Africa to Asia, Cabot's and Vespucci's explorations along the coasts of the Americas, culminating in Magellan's crew's circumnavigation of the globe. The explorers responsible for these discoveries often returned from their odysseys laden with exotic animals to be presented as gifts to their patrons, and always bursting with stories:

> In Bactria are trees that bear wool, as though it were of sheep, whereof men make clothes, and all things that may be made of wool. In that country too are many 'ipotaynes' that dwell sometimes on the land, and sometimes in the water, and they are half man and half horse, and they eat men when they take them. And in that country are many griffins. Some men say that they have the body upward of an eagle, and beneath of a lion, and that is true!

And here is the same writer, Sir John Mandeville, a little later in his voyage:

> In that great wilderness are the trees of the Sun and the Moon, that told King Alexander of his death. The people that eat the fruit and the balm live four or five hundred years. . . . My companions and I would gladly have gone there but for the great number of wild beasts that are in that wilderness, like dragons, serpents and other ravening beasts that eat all they can get. There are many elephants, all white; some are

blue, and of other colours, quite numberless. There are also many unicorns and lions and other hideous beasts.

When travelers like the St Albans–born Mandeville returned to England from their voyages to far-flung parts of the world, telling tales of wonders they had seen, or even bringing with them pictures of peculiar things, wild beasts or magical places, few had the knowledge to question the veracity of their claims. Who was to say that elephants weren't also available in blue, or that there was no country called Bactria where griffins abound? How many people in London had ever seen an elephant, or been to the Indies themselves? All one could hope to learn from the maps of these places was that here be monsters, or here be dragons. No one possessed the personal experience that might call into question these fabulous stories, and few could follow Münchausen's advice – 'let him take a voyage there himself' – so these accounts became the only authority – and therefore the gospel truth. Anyone back in England who had any awareness of the existence of elephants at all had only secondhand information, either from explorers' tall tales or from a bestiary. Mandeville says elephants are blue, and that they live near the lions and unicorns, and he's been there so he should know.

Just as the Bible was to be believed unquestioningly, and respected unquestioningly, there was a strong tradition of respect for the authority of the classical writers. It was in part this credulity that led to errors in the *Physiologus* being imported unchecked into medieval bestiaries. And this faith in the printed word – a misplaced faith perhaps – even stretched to cover the words of Mandeville.

Other highlights of Mandeville's travels include the Fountain of Youth, an animal called a chameleon that 'neither eats nor drinks, but goes along always with its mouth open for it lives on air,' and six-footed bears with lions' tails. We might just have to admit that these accounts, popular as they were, were not the most reliable of evidence.

Now the fact that (just as it happens) Mandeville almost certainly never existed would seem at first to account for this element of fantasy – after all, anyone (now) can tell that *The Travels of Sir John Mandeville* is in fact nothing more than a medieval romance, a hoax, an elaborate fiction written by some (French) historian. Surely no one would be foolish enough to believe in such things?

And yet his descriptions are no more fantastical or seemingly embellished than those of any contemporary traveler. Marco Polo's *Travels* include descriptions of men with dogs' heads and accounts of another race, 'adepts beyond all others in the art of magic; insomuch that they can compel their idols, although by nature dumb and deaf, to speak; they can likewise obscure the day, and perform many other miracles' (not to mention the excesses of Kubla Khan's menagerie, accounted one of the marvels of the day). And not only did Marco Polo quite definitely exist – no one would question that nowadays – but he is still regarded as a more or less respectable source in his way.* When

---

* Though some questions have recently been raised as to whether he traveled at all. Part of the case against him rests on the fact that his accounts of his time and travels in China fail entirely to mention the Great Wall, which had probably been completed by that time. The argument is examined in an article by T. H. Barret, entitled simply 'Wall? I Saw No Wall.'

Shakespeare satirizes this belief in tall tales, having Othello tell the naïve young Desdemona of the things he has seen in his 'travel's history,' 'of the Cannibals that each other eat, / The Anthropophagi, and men whose heads / Do grow beneath their shoulders,' his character is in the very best company. And, frankly, it's no wonder the girl is impressed.

Dozens of copies of Marco Polo's *Travels* circulated Europe in manuscript. And of course he too was believed when he brought his stories home (lions with red and white stripes, etc.). Who was there who could contradict him?*

The same applies to the most famous explorer-discoverer of them all. When in 1492 Christopher Columbus (in the *Niña*, the *Pinta* and the *Santa Maria*) made his famous crossing of the Atlantic, he recorded in his diary his encounters with animal oddities. These include not only such curiosities as a fish 'that looked just like a pig, not like a porpoise,' which he says 'was all hard shell and had nothing soft except the tail and the eyes and a hole underneath for expelling its superfluities' (which he dutifully had 'salted to take to Spain so the sovereigns could see it') but also on 4 November a place where 'there were one-eyed men, and others,

---

* There are of course a number of explanations for the appearance of such anomalies in stories like Marco Polo's, stories purporting to be entirely true; without going into them in too much detail, it is worth considering briefly that there may have been good reasons for Polo having written what he did. Was he actually told of these things, and foolish enough to believe in them himself? Was he embellishing things a little to impress people (potential sponsors, perhaps?), or trying to explain things he himself did not understand? Or when a native was trying to explain what was what, was something simply lost in translation?

with snouts of dogs, who ate men, and that as soon as one was taken they cut his throat and drank his blood and cut off his genitals.'* He didn't, admittedly, see such things himself, but certainly 'understood' that they existed, following some communication with the local inhabitants.

Now, Columbus arrived in the New World with a ship well stocked in interpreters, but unfortunately only with interpreters who spoke Hebrew, Arabic, Aramaic (Chaldean), Portuguese, Spanish and of course Italian, none of which will have been of much use in communicating with the natives. Aramaic? Is it any wonder the natives' sign language was misinterpreted? But if that was the case, what meaning could they possibly have been trying to communicate? Or did he interpret their gestures correctly, and they were just trying to scare him?

Columbus returned to Spain the following March, with parrots and macaws as souvenirs for King Ferdinand and Queen Isabella (anything to keep them sweet and make them more likely to fund another journey, and another). It was already traditional for explorers to bring live souvenirs home to enhance their patrons' menageries. One great explorer who was prevented from doing this was the Spaniard Hernán Cortés; in 1520 he attacked and besieged the Aztec capital of Tenochtitlán, a city in part famous for its vast menagerie belonging to the magnificent emperor Montezuma (a menagerie so vast it required a mind-boggling six

---

* Incidentally, according to current estimates of his progress, he is believed to have been somewhere on the north coast of Cuba when he reported these wonders on 4 November.

hundred keepers).* As the fighting intensified, the tempers of the Aztec warriors became more heated and they threatened to throw the invading Spaniards to the animals. During the very long siege that followed many of the native inhabitants of the city did manage to survive the invasion, but it did become necessary for the contents of the zoo to be eaten. Cortés would have to look elsewhere for animals to bring back with him when he finally returned to Europe eight years later.

When Columbus was summoned to Barcelona on 20 April 1493 to report to Ferdinand and Isabella, he gave them a copy of his diary. They would have had no reason not to believe its tales implicitly, just as those who listened to his stories over a cup of wine late into the night in a dimly lit bar in Seville or Córdoba must have sat rapt, believing their every fabulous word.

And just as readily the English believed the probably fictional Mandeville, and his travels became widely popular, being translated into every European language. There are some three hundred manuscript copies still extant, with examples in every major European library. Almost three hundred years after the appearance of *The Travels of Sir John Mandeville*, Richard Brome – manservant-cum-secretary to Ben Jonson – wrote a play called *The Antipodes*, about a man whose reading of Mandeville has made him obsessed with the idea of travel. Peregrine's distressed family

OVERLEAF   *'Here be dragons': map of the world by Pierre Desceliers, 1546.*

---

* Compared with under a hundred at London Zoo today.

even sent him to a kind of psychiatrist (and bear in mind that this was written in 1638) to try to cure him of this obsession:

> Pray, Dr Hughball,
> Play the man-midwife and deliver him
> Of his huge tympany of news – of monsters,
> Pygmies and giants, apes and elephants,
> Gryphons and crocodiles . . .

But the comedy in this play is not at the expense of a man who cannot distinguish travel writing from fantasy literature, for none of Brome's audience could have had any more idea than the over-enthusiastic Peregrine that Mandeville was a fake, and that elephants vary from place to place and species to species only in their shades of gray and the size of their ears. Nor, for that matter, could Brome. Questions had begun to be asked about the authenticity of these unlikely tales, but even now the consensus was still for their veracity. No less a man than Sir Walter Ralegh declared that – though he had had his doubts in the past – he was quite sure now that it was all true: '[Mandeville's] reports were holden for fables many yeeres, and yet since the East Indies were discovered, we find his relations true of such things as heretofore were held incredible.'* In other words, we have reliable proof that blue elephants do exist after all. How reassuring to learn that Mandeville must have been telling the truth all along. There were of course people who did doubt the

---

* This avowal of faith appeared in Ralegh's *Discoverie of Guiana*, which also included fables of the city of El Dorado, but we can let that pass.

veracity of reports of unicorns and the like, but Edward Topsell suggests this was because they had trouble believing in 'any beast but such as is in their own flocks.' In other words lions, elephants and their ilk may have been equally suspect.

The reliance of the English people on other people's stories and pictures of animals ended in the 1420s, with the arrival of visitors to the Menagerie. Not just anyone could walk in off the streets, of course, for this was still at least in name one of the king's homes. So it is likely that the matter of who was to be let in had more to do with connections than the ability or willingness to pay any kind of fixed admission fee. From now on, foreigners (tourists, traders, diplomats) with suitable letters of introduction, officials of all kinds, Londoners who were friends of the Right People or related to them, had exclusive access to the king's animals, and a two-century head start on the ineligible remainder of the population.

So long as you were the Right Sort of Person, then, if you wanted to know what a tiger looked like, whether the picture in your book was accurate, you could march straight over to the Tower and check for yourself – you could see one *with your own eyes*. Indeed, if you owned books at all the chances are that you were indeed such an eligible person. And those who could not afford the 3 sous admission fee, or who chose not to pay it (this was not a small amount of money), could choose the alternative payment plan. A decree by Henry VI meant that free admission was given to anyone willing to offer their dog or cat (or presumably by extension horses, sheep, etc.) as a contribution towards the lions' dinner. If you timed it right you might even be able to watch the feeding. The kids must have loved it.

There was no contradiction in this. Certain animals – domestic animals, farm animals – were still regarded as nothing more than commodities. Exotic animals were a quite different matter – lions had more in common with dragons, bears, mermaids or unicorns ('other hideous beasts,' Mandeville had said) than with cats. Cats were two a penny (perhaps even literally?), good only for catching mice (and feeding to lions); the public were only interested in really unfamiliar animals, and fierce ones too, if at all possible.* Wolves, for instance, had lately been commonplace all over England (as recently as the thirteenth century Hampstead Heath had been overrun with them), but as soon as they began to disappear from the English countryside they suddenly became exciting and glamorous and began to appear on show in the Tower. There were almost none to be found in the wild by the late fifteenth century, and by 1599 Thomas Platter was describing the Tower's 'lean, ugly wolf' as 'the only one in England.'

Admittedly the selection of animals during the reign of Henry VI was still fairly limited. Lions and other big cats were (as they almost always are) the public's favorites, which may be why from this period the post of keeper, which William de Botton had occupied two centuries earlier, became known as 'Keeper of the Lions, Lionesses and Leopards Within the Tower of London.' As

---

* Echoes of this in the 1997 film *Fierce Creatures*, in which a public zoo threatened with closure is forced to dispose of any animals not sufficiently fierce. 'I'll tell you,' says the new boss, 'exactly what draws the biggest audiences all over the world: Violence. Therefore in this zoo we require only animals which are potentially violent. All the rest, I'm afraid, will have to go.' Five hundred years earlier, the first public zoo in the country was already using violence to sell tickets.

a rule this title was bestowed for life; although William Kerby, the official who had been appointed by the king's father, Henry V, was one of the few who did not die on the job. He was actually stripped of his title (after a perfectly honorable twenty-three years in charge), as he was unfortunate enough to be presiding when in 1436 the lions in the Menagerie died. All of them.

No satisfactory explanation has yet been given for this. All we have is a record in *The Chronicle of London* that 'deyde all the lyons that were in the Tour of London whiche was nought seen in no mannys tyme before out of mynde.' Certainly an element of curatorial incompetence is likely to have had something to do with this mass death; the very fact that the Tower housed only interesting and exotic animals was all but a guarantee that your average English keeper knew as little about them as your average London visitor. In any case they all died, within the space of a few months, of disease, or malnutrition, or something equally efficient. Out went William Kerby in disgrace, and in came Robert Manfeld, marshal of the King's Hall, with a starting salary of 6*d* a day, an apartment at the Tower (though admittedly not one he liked much – he found it 'Ruynous'), and responsibility for maintaining a glorious royal Menagerie with two hundred years of history and tradition behind it, and containing not one single animal.

It was not until 1445 that anything was done to remedy this sorry situation. In a satisfying echo of the story of the Menagerie's first inhabitants the turnaround came with the king's marriage into European royalty. Where Henry III had married his sister into one of Europe's most powerful families, Henry VI himself was now set to marry, and the object of this policy decision was the young French princess Margaret of Anjou. Margaret (who was later to become the magnificent battle-axe queen of Shake-speare's history plays) had, unlike Henry, been born into a family of real animal enthusiasts – her father René had a spectacular collection at his fairy-tale castle in Saumur and the neighbouring château at Angers. Knowing of this history, one of Henry's courtiers sought to curry favor with Margaret by bringing her a lion to Titchfield Abbey as a wedding present, perhaps thinking it might help to make the sixteen-year-old feel at home. By all accounts she was delighted, as was her new husband; one 'John Fouke of Peryn' was appointed to convey it to the Tower, and the Menagerie was back in business, with Manfeld finally earning his keep by supervising the rebuilding of the enclosures and the acquisition of a new and growing collection.

Until then the records for Manfeld in the Patent Rolls had been rather different from the dozen or so preceding him – necessarily, as he was the only keeper who had had no animals in his charge. The first half of the entry follows the familiar pattern, but it ends with a proviso: 'Provided always that the said Robert, by force of this grant, do not take and wages, fees, profits or easements, except the accustomed houses for the keeper and lions, unless there be actually lions in the Tower as there have been in the past.' When this was amended two years later, a further security meas-ure was added. The fees would stand 'provided always that the Chancellor of England shall have power to examine him or his deputy upon oath as to the number of beasts in their charge.'

Another six years later, the pay had risen from 6*d* to 12*d* (and generously backdated a few months), and security had slipped a little; now the entry reads, rather casually, that the chancellor would retain the power to question him 'from time to time.' All of which must have been moot since at this point Manfeld still had not seen a single animal brought into his care, as he wouldn't till the Anjou marriage a year later. When this did at last happen, he may have felt unable to cope with the unexpected rigors of the job, for he was joined in the position by his son Richard, and following Richard's death by his other son Robert. Between them they held the keepership for a quarter of a century.

As the Wars of the Roses drew towards their close in the early 1480s, and the Tower passed from the hands of the Lancasters (it had remained loyal to Henry VI throughout) to the Yorkists, the position of keeper attracted men of a quite different caliber. Sir Robert Brakenbury, who appears in Shakespeare's *Richard III* as the trusted lieutenant of the Tower (first under Edward IV, at the start of the play, then under Richard), was appointed by Richard, the last Yorkist king, as the jailer of the two kings' brother Clarence and later of the young, soon-to-be-murdered princes. The keeping of the animals was clearly a titular post – an honor, and little else, with all the real work being done by Sir Robert's minions. He would himself have been too busy defending the capital against the arrival of the first Tudor king, the man who would soon be Henry VII.

Richard's reign was short (mercifully short, if you believe Shakespeare's portrayal of him), and accordingly so was Brakenbury's tenure at the Tower. After the Battle of Bosworth Field and Richard's death in 1485, the new King Henry appointed to the position of keeper John, the earl of Oxford (referred to in the grant as 'the king's kinsman'), another veteran of

Shakespeare's history plays. On the same day, John was appointed constable of the Tower, traditionally a high honor too, but also a *real* job, well suited to a man of his station.

Despite granting the position of keeper to his loyal kinsman, it may be that Henry was a little ambivalent towards the Menagerie in the Tower. He certainly visited it, but found the spectacle of a lion beset by mastiffs there most displeasing. John Caius, in his *Of English Dogges*, reported that:

> Henry the seventh of that name, King of England (a Prince both Politic and warlike) . . . commanded all such dogs (how many soever there were in number) should be hanged, being deeply displeased, and conceiving great disdain, that an ill-favoured rascal cur should with such villainy, assault the valiant Lion, King of all beasts.

Any potentially rebellious subjects take note.

The Tower was fast approaching the most notorious phase in its history; the reigns of Henry's son Henry VIII (the great Lion himself)* and his children would prove fraught with religious divisions, and the Tower found itself symbolically at the heart of the troubles, housing the out-of-favor in its cells. Henry VIII's lieutenant of the Tower, Sir Edward Walsingham (uncle to Francis

---

* Sir Thomas More wrote: 'You often boast to me that you have the king's ear and often have fun with him, freely and according to your whims. This is like having fun with tamed lions – often it is harmless, but just as often there is fear of harm. Often he roars in rage for no known reason, and suddenly the fun becomes fatal.'

Walsingham, the man who was to become Elizabeth I's great spy-master), would supervise the custody of a queen, senior clergy and countless other noteworthy subjects.

Yet throughout the fifteenth and sixteenth centuries public visits to the Tower do not appear to have stopped at all; visitors were allowed at least as far as the Lion Tower, while a stone's throw away Sir Thomas More was being prepared for his martyrdom, or a few days later John Fisher was readying himself for his. Just as we presume that fifty years earlier not only were the royal princes taken to see the animals in the Tower, but also that other visitors were allowed in during the boys' own sad days of imprisonment there. The Tower had many faces, and they were often hard to reconcile.

But for visitors it was a simple matter. In this period they were, by modern standards, a pretty easy bunch to please. Just as London Zoo today swarms with children who get a particular thrill from seeing things they've never seen before (unlike all the rather jaded parents or baby-sitters who have been doing this for years . . .), so everything in the Tower Menagerie was new to its visitors; the ten-year hiatus following the mass death in 1436 had just meant that there was another generation growing up who had never yet seen a living lion, and who would certainly be prepared to pay for the privilege of doing so. The animals on display were some of God's most magnificent works, some of the masterpieces of the Creator's art — just imagine seeing a tiger for the

OVERLEAF   *More dragons: Jan van Doetecum's map of the North Atlantic, c. 1594.*

Secundùm littora Novæ Franciæ multæ in sicum imn: quæ Balena.

Hope Sanderson

GROENLANT

Serehn gers.

Alba

OCEANUS DEUCALIDONIUS

OCEANUS GERMANICUS

Bruges

OCEANUS HISPANICUS

Islas Maidas

Asores Insulæ al: Flandricæ

Nova Francia, alio nomine dicta Terra nova, anno 1504. à Britonibus primum detecta circa sinum S. Laurentij, & anno 1524. à Ioanne Verrazzano Florentino, qui ex portu Diepensi 17 Martij, soluens nomine Francisci Regis Galliarum ibidem appulit ad gradum 34. circiter latitudinis siue altitudinis Polæ, plenius recognita usque ad promontorium dictum Cabo de Breton.

OCEANUS ATLAN

Insulæ Canariæ ol. Fortunatæ

TICUS

first time! No one who could afford it, or who could spare one of their own or their children's pets in lieu of the admission fee, would have hesitated to head for Tower Hill to stare in awe at them, and marvel at His genius.

But what should these beasts be fed? Why has He designed them as He has? How do they live in the wild? Needless to say, at this time such enquiry into the workings of the Tower's animals was out of the question. That is, it simply would not have occurred to a fifteenth-century Londoner. Magic is magic, just as faith is faith, and there is no explanation for it – or perhaps it was just that finding an explanation would detract from what made it magic. This argument continued throughout the Enlightenment and far beyond. Keats was famously disparaging of the influence of Isaac Newton, who, he said, had 'destroyed all the poetry of the rainbow by reducing it to a Prism.' Surely the rainbow, and other such phenomena considered 'sublime' by the English Romantics, were best left unexplained? Natural science of sorts had been done in Europe for many centuries (remember Aristotle, and Frederick's book on falcons), but stubborn, magic-struck little England showed remarkably little curiosity until well into the eighteenth century – which of course explains why until then none of the Tower's animals lived very long.

It was a combination of the very gradual waning of magic and the consolidation of religious beliefs that delayed advances in these disciplines, and maintained the English in a state of quite remarkable credulity where matters of 'natural philosophy' were concerned. By the Enlightenment it could be acknowledged that magic and religion had both been forms of pre-science, in that both were created to fill the role that – certain developmental stages later – science would come to occupy. In the absence of better explanations for baffling phenomena, magical or mythological or religious explanations step in to fill the breach, and gain considerable currency. Even men like Newton saw their science as a way of understanding *God's* creation. The world is perfectly ordered and explicable, which is proof that God *does* exist. All of which made those distinctions between what is real and what is not – in this case, which animals do actually exist? – just that little bit more tricky to draw.

By 1552, the word 'exotic' has its first recorded usage, finding its way into the work of Rabelais ('exotique'), and crossing over to England later that same century – Ben Jonson for one used it in 1599, in his *Every Man Out of His Humour*; and as the word arrived so, with it, did the whole idea of exoticism. And the idea of exoticism helped to resolve the problem, as it defines those things that are odd and foreign (and probably inexplicable) but still real.

To some extent it was becoming possible to draw (reasonably accurate) distinctions between what was unquestionably real and what might not be. The Menagerie, with its live specimens, fulfilled the role of a sort of prescientific laboratory. Nobody was consciously conducting experiments, not at this stage, and yet empirical evidence of sorts was being gathered and doubts resolved, if only by casual or accidental observation. It would be simplistic and misleading to suggest that the difference made by the Menagerie was the bringing of enlightenment where once there had been only the shadows of ignorance, but it is true that at least some kinds of discernment were *possible*, for the first time, even if not widespread.

As this discernment began to spread, slowly, and as it became easier and easier to see live exotic animals, so it became clear that bestiaries had had their day. In the twelfth and thirteenth centuries the bestiary had been one of the most widely known books (after the Bible), found in all good monastic libraries; by the sixteenth it was all but obsolete. Who needs bestiaries when you have the real thing?

4

Fun and Games

The King, Queene, and Prince, the Lady Elizabeth, and the Duke of Yorke, with divers great Lords, and manie others, came to the Tower to see a triall of the Lyons single valour, against a great fierce Beare which had kild a child that was negligently left in the Beare-House. This fierce Beare was brought into the open yard, behind the Lyons Den, which was the place for the fight: then was the great Lyon put forth, who gazed a while, but never offred to assault or approch the Beare: then were two mastife Dogs put in, who past by the Beare, and boldly seazed upon the Lyon . . . [And on 5 July, two weeks and eight lions later:] According to the kings commandement, this Beare was bayted to death upon a stage: and unto the mother of the murthered child was given xx.p., out of part of that money which the people gave to see the Beare Kild.

—John Stow, 1609

For an animal that was not indigenous to the British Isles, it is surprising to discover just how many brown bears were on view in London at the start of the seventeenth century. Unlike Henry III's charismatic polar bear, which as you may remember we left sitting in the sun on Tower Wharf, brown bears were, if not commonplace, certainly no great rarity. It was the brutal sport of bear-baiting that created most of the demand for these imports. The unfortunate animals were chained, usually toothless, to a post in a yard and mastiff dogs set on them, with punters watching in awe at the violence and bloodshed and taking bets on which species would do the most damage. On the south bank of the Thames, where such sports had long been a common sight, the turnover in bears was very high indeed.*

One of the great organizers of this practice was the actor and impresario Edward Alleyn. Alleyn was son-in-law to the theatre-manager Philip Henslowe and the leading actor in Henslowe's company, the Admiral's Men. With this company, based at the Rose Theatre, Alleyn created many of the greatest roles of his day – Marlowe's Faustus, Tamburlaine, the Jew of Malta; it has been claimed, too, that he may have created Shakespeare's Mercutio, but the theory is unfounded, whatever the film *Shakespeare in Love* may tell you. Before his retirement to Dulwich† (where in 1619 he founded Dulwich College with some of his personal fortune – amassed mainly in his work as an impresario rather than as an actor – how little things change) he had performed at court for Queen Elizabeth and then King James, and

---

* At one point the Paris Garden alone had twenty bears (not to mention three bulls and seventy mastiffs).

† Mostly spent with his scandalously young second wife, Constance, daughter of Dr John Donne, the poet and dean of St Paul's.

Bear-baiting, from an early-seventeenth-century German woodcut.

been acclaimed in a sonnet by Ben Jonson that compared him to Roscius and Cicero ('who both their graces in thyself hast more outstripped'), ending with the couplet

> Wear this renown: 'Tis just, that who did give
> So many poets life, by one should live.

But Alleyn's renown was not quite as grand and lofty as Jonson suggests; it was certainly not all great tragedy and the noble creation of high art.

Just alongside Henslowe's base at the Rose was another of his going concerns, the Hope Theatre, on a site where today you will find an alley by the name of Bear Gardens. The Hope was used only rarely for plays but frequently for animal-baiting. In the Braun and Hogenberg map of around 1572, the building is unnamed – it merely says 'bear bayting,' the building next door 'Bolle Bayting,' as bulls were the second most frequently baited commodity in the area.* Audiences thronged to these events – like his father-in-law, Mr Alleyn was known to be good at giving the public what they wanted. So it was Alleyn and Henslowe whom the new King James appointed joint masters of the Royal Game of Bears, Bulls and Mastiff Dogs in 1604 (in fact, to be quite accurate, it was not Alleyn and Henslowe who were first given this title, but the chosen incumbent was more than willing to sell it on to them for a comfortable profit); and it was Alleyn whom the king called upon in March of that year to supply good fighting dogs to test the mettle of his new African lion.† Strong, burly and tenacious dogs were artificially bred for this sport, trained to sink their teeth into a bull's nose and not let go; these delightful creatures were called, of course, bulldogs.

---

* It has been suggested that this concurrence of Bears and Bulls has given us the terminology used to describe stock markets, whereby a bear (a pessimistic market) drags you down in a struggle, and a bull (an optimistic market) will hurl you up into the air.

† It was not long before the keeper of the animals in the Tower had acquired his own stock of mastiffs for this purpose; by the time Samuel Kiechel visited from Germany in 1585, he claimed (with what is probably only a small degree of exaggeration) to have seen 250 such dogs housed there.

Fun and Games

OVERLEAF   *Braun and Hogenberg's map of London, 1572. 'The Towre' is easily seen at the far right, with the little semicircular Lion Tower making up its bottom lefthand (SW) corner.*

It would hardly have been appropriate for the king to attend a baiting in a bearpit, especially one on the wrong side of the river; after all, the city authorities were trying to stamp out such disagreeable behavior.* But similar displays of valor and bloodletting in a royal palace were quite another matter. This was perhaps not inappropriate; though not a permanent royal home (like Elizabeth before him James had chosen not to live there under normal circumstances) the Tower was still in regular use as a place of imprisonment and execution; residents at the time included the unfortunate and much-imprisoned Walter Ralegh (the man who believed Mandeville), lodged with his family in the Bloody Tower, less than a hundred yards from the animal pens. And besides being a regular hunter, the king was more than commonly interested in sporting bloodshed, always insisting on disemboweling the final kill of the hunt himself, and even performing a kind of blood rite whereby he would daub his courtiers with the blood of the kill, and the ladies of the household would dip their hands in it, apparently 'supposing it will make them white.'

For years the Tower Menagerie had prided itself on its collection of wild, carnivorous (and thus sharper-toothed) creatures; and it may have seemed to the king that an opportunity was being wasted. Why, after all, need he import a south-of-the-river brown

---

* Though in fact on at least one occasion Queen Elizabeth I had attended the Southwark Bear Gardens, when she took the Spanish ambassador in 1575.

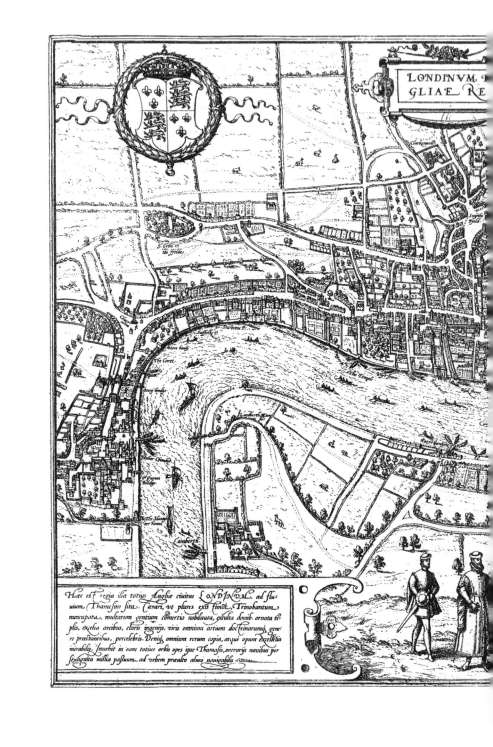

LONDINVM
GLIAE RE

Clarkenwell

S. Gyles in
the fylde

Suffolke P.

Durinus F.

The Bere bayting

The Corte

The Quens
Bridge

Paris Gardin
or Bettes houfe

Lambeth

Hæc est regia illa totius Angliæ ciuitas LONDINVM. ad flu-
uium Thamefim fita. Cæsari, vt plures exiſt fimãt, Trinobantum
nuncupata, multarum gentium comertio nobilitata, exculta domib. ornata tē-
plis, excelsa arcibus, claris ingenijs, viris omnium artium doctrinarumq̃, gene-
re præstantibus, percelebris. Deniq̃, omnium rerum copia, atq́ue opum excellétia
mirabilis. Inuehit in eam totius orbis opes ipse Thamaſis, onerarijs nauibus per
sexaginta millia paſſuum, ad vrbem prealto alueo nauigabilis.

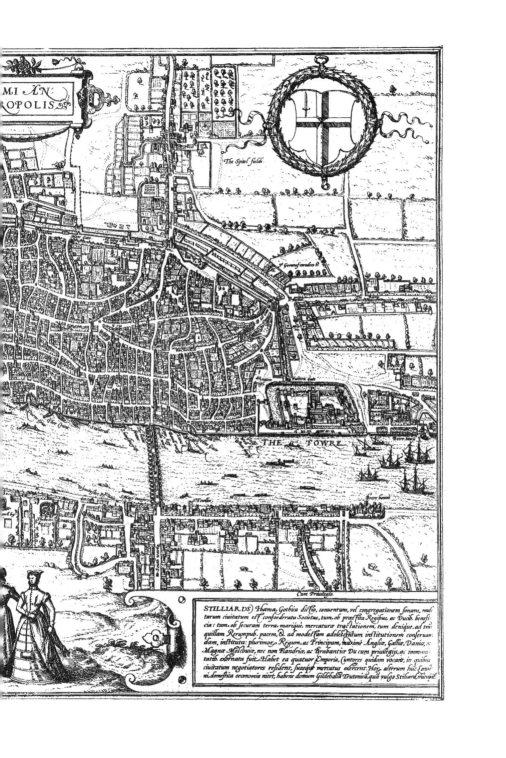

MI AN
OPOLIS

The Spitel fields

THE · TOWRE

Cum Priuilegio.

STILLIARDS) Hansa, Gothica dictio, conuentum, vel congregationem sonans, multarum ciuitatum est confoederata Societas, tum, ob praestita Regibus, ac Ducib. beneficia: tum, ob securam terra, mariqui. mercaturae tractlationem, tum denique, ad tranquillam Rerumpub. pacem, & ad modestam adolescentum institutionem conseruandam, instituta: plurimor. Regum, ac Principum, maxime Angliae, Galliae, Daniae, ac Magnae Moscouiae, nec non Flandriae, ac Brabantiae Du cum priuilegijs, ac immunitatib. exornata fuit. Habet ea quatuor Emporia, (untores quidam vocant, in quibus ciuitatum negotiatores resident, suosque mercatus exerent. Hor. alterum heic: alteroni. domestica oeconomia nitet, habens domum Gildehalla Teutonica, quá vulgo Stilliard, nuncur.

bear to fight, when he had leopards of his own, not to mention lions and tigers and bears (oh my)? And why only mastiffs? Why not pit wildcats against each other, lions against lions, or against tigers or leopards? Or for that matter against bears? Horses? Sheep? The more exotic animals were valuable, it is true, enormously awkward and costly to replace if badly damaged, but they had such great entertainment potential.

In the previous century the Portuguese king had decided to pit an elephant and a rhinoceros against each other to test their relative strengths and assess the level of their animosity. But he was never able to ascertain which was the stronger, for no sooner had the young elephant taken one look at his fearsome opponent than he went hurtling out of the arena, trying to make a bid for freedom, plunging into the Lisbon streets without a backward glance.

It's hard to blame the elephant for his spirited attempt at escape, but one can't help feeling that England's King James wouldn't have been impressed. He got far better behavior and more satisfactory results when he stuck to lions and dogs, neither one a species known for its timidity. So on the morning of 13 March 1604, Alleyn had a small consignment of his fiercest mastiffs delivered to the keeper Ralph Gill at the Tower to fight the king's lion. That afternoon the new king, well attended, arrived at the Lion Tower, eager to see a good bit of lively entertainment; Edward Alleyn, the consummate showman, was just the man to oblige.

13 March 1604

The King, being told of the lions in the Tower, asked how they came thither, for in England there are bred no such fierce beasts. To which answer was given that the mastiff dog

is of as great courage as the lion. Hereupon the King caused
Mr Edward Alleyn, now sworne the Prince's man, and
Master of the Bear Garden, to fetch secretly three of the
fellest dogs in the Garden. Which being done, the King, the
Queen and the Prince went secretly to the Lion's tower, and
caused the fellest lion to be separated from his mate, and one
dog alone put in the lion's den, who straightway flew to the
face of the lion. But the lion shook him off, and grasped him
fast by the neck, drawing the dog upstairs and downstairs.
The King, now perceiving the lion greatly exceed the dog in
strength, but nothing in noble heart and courage, caused
another dog to be put into the den, who likewise took the
lion by the face, and he began to deal with him as with the
former; but whilst he held them both under his paws they bit
him by the belly, whereat the lion roared so extremely that
the earth shook withal; and the next lion ramped and roared
as if he would have made rescue. The third dog was then put
in and likewise took the lion by the lip . . .

—John Stow

Because of their long association with royalty, with royal crests,
valor and so forth, there was never any challenge to the lion's
status as King of the Beasts. In the hierarchy that was the animal
kingdom (as then perceived), the lion's right to the title went
without question. (Of course when national pride was at stake it
was a different matter altogether; it was maintained with commendable patriotism that a British mastiff was no less noble or
brave than an African lion, being, after all, British.) And in such
high esteem was the lion held that other animals could become

nobler merely by association. In this case, though two of the three
mastiffs involved in the fight with the lion died (one in the pit
during the fight, one subsequently of its injuries), the survivor –
alive but doubtless rather shaken – was adopted by Henry, the
young and surprisingly enlightened Prince of Wales. The prince,
who as it happens had his own private collection of animals
housed at St James's Palace – which included, distressingly, 'a
rare Indian bird called an emu that can devour burning coals' –
took to this dog on the grounds that it had battled the King of the
Beasts and survived. As a reward for its bravery, 'the Prince hath
commanded [Alleyn] that he [the dog] shall be sent to St James'
and there kept and made much of, saying that he that hath
fought with the King of Beasts shall never fight with any inferior
creature.'

Although King James, unlike his son, harbored no romantic
notions of animal honor and respect (or perhaps precisely for
this reason), he quickly acquired a taste for such sport. And later
the same year, with his own viewing convenience in mind, he
ordered the complete reconstruction of the Lion Tower as a semi-
circular structure, bounded on the outside curve by the Tower's
now partially drained moat. This new outer area was surrounded
by a wall built to enclose it from the moat and the land outside
Tower grounds, and this served as an exercise yard for the animals, which (according to one chronicler) 'shall be maintayned
and kept for speciall place to baight the Lyons with dogges,
beares, bulles, bores, etc.'

This spring of the yeare, the king builded a wall, and filled
up with earth, all that part of the mote or ditch, round about

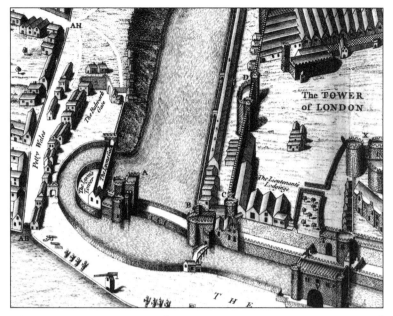

The Lion Tower; a detail taken from Haiward and Gascoyne's 1597 plan of the Tower complex.

the West side of the Lyons den, and appointed a drawing partition to be made towards the South part thereof, the one part thereof to serve for the breeding Lionesse: when she shall have whelps, and the other part thereof, for a walke for other Lions. The king caused also three trap dores to bee made in the wall of the Lyons den, for the Lyons to goe into their walke, at the pleasure of their keeper.

—John Stow

There were now steps for the animals to move easily from one level of their den to the other, a water trough in the yard 'for the

Lyons to drinke and washe themselfes in' and an area for them to be fed. At this time the Butchers' Company would supply offal for the king's bears and other animals, which would arrive by boat at the arenas on Bankside before continuing downriver to the Tower. The stench of these vast quantities of low-quality, ageing offal, progressing slowly east along the main thoroughfare of the city, especially in the hot summer months, was legendary. Trying to describe a particularly noxious smell, around 1610, Ben Jonson could think of no more extreme comparison than to say that

> The meat-boat of Bears' college, Paris garden,
> Stunk not so ill; (nor when she kissed, Kate Arden).

At the king's command the new design included the added feature of a special wooden viewing platform high above the enclosure, designed to have the most comfortable sightlines over the animal yard, 'for the kinges Maiestie to stande on to see the Lyons lett out.'

By this time the Menagerie had grown to cover most of the area it was to occupy until its closure over three hundred years later.

The work was completed early the following year. In no time at all, animals were regularly set fighting there; or when this was not possible they were occasionally — as a concession to the blood-thirsty — fed live meals; so that even if there were no fights arranged for an afternoon, a tourist could still hope to see a sheep or a cock being ripped apart, at the very least. Not quite a majestic battle between the valiant King of the Beasts and a magnificent

Indian tiger, but it was still exciting and bloody, and at least it was cheap.

3 June 1605

This afternoon his majesty, being accompanied with divers noblemen and many knights and gentlemen, came to the Lions' Tower. Then Mr Ralph Gill, keeper of the lions, was commanded that his servants should put forth into the walk the male and female breeder, but the lions would not go out until they were forced out with burning links, when they stood looking about in amazement. Then were two racks of mutton thrown down to them, which they straightway ate. Then a lusty live cock was cast down, which they killed and sucked his blood; and then another live cock which they likewise killed but sucked not.

—John Stow

With the two cocks destroyed (not to mention the two racks of mutton as a meager appetizer), it seems that the king was still not satisfied; but these spectacles were not always as bloodily predictable as their organizers might have hoped, and what followed is perhaps not what he had had in mind:

After that the King caused a live lamb to be easily let down by a rope, but the lions stood in their place and only beheld the lamb. But the lamb rose up and went towards the lions, who very gently looked upon him and smelled on him without sign of any further hurt. Then the lamb was softly drawn up again in as good plight as he was set down.

Hmm (you can almost hear him thinking), let's try again . . .

> Then they caused these lions to be put into their den, and another lion to be put forth and two lusty mastiffs at a by-door to be let unto him. These flew fiercely upon him, and perceiving the lion's neck to be defended with hair they sought only to bite him by the face. Then was a third dog let in, as fierce as either let in, a brended dog, that took the lion by the face and turned him upon his back; but the lion spoiled them all.

Yes, that's *much* better.

Such cruelty (or at least what we recognize as cruelty these days) was not at all unusual. But since the end of the Middle Ages such extremes of inhumanity were generally confined to the treatment of animals; on the whole torture of humans was at this time neither current nor acceptable by 'common law' (apparently the burning of heretics didn't really count). Exceptions to this general rule were authorized only in cases of particularly seditious treason; one such incident took place in this same year of 1605, on Tuesday, 5 November, in the cellars of Parliament. The man arrested (caught *in flagrante* in the cellars, a lantern in hand, a look of desperate panic on his face), Guy Fawkes, was taken to the Tower, where he was brutally tortured for several days. Visitors to the lions in mid-November would doubtless have heard, above the roaring and growling, the sounds of 'John Johnson' (Fawkes's alias in this enterprise) being stretched on the rack in the next building. This treatment of Fawkes and his coconspirators did not sit easily on the conscience of Londoners, except for the few most vehemently anti-Catholic. At least with animals, James could feel sure that the people of London were unlikely to become suddenly and uncharacteristically scrupulous or squeamish.

It was largely taken for granted that such animals – indeed, all animals – existed merely to meet a need of mankind, providing meat, brute strength or entertainment. Londoners would still have accepted readily that such things had been put on earth for us alone – this is, after all, a time when what we now call 'Humanism' was still the prevailing worldview. There may have been some elementary enquiry into the functioning of animals by now, but this was invariably in order to determine how one might best use the information acquired to benefit humanity. So when, for example, Francis Bacon (a well-connected man who would doubtless have had access to the Tower Menagerie) wrote his *New Atlantis*, the idealized institution he imagined in it – a kind of scientific college, called Salomon's House – included animal collections among its other facilities. Our guide explains:

> We have also parks and inclosures of all sorts of beasts and birds, which we use not only for view or rareness, but likewise for dissections and trials; that thereby we may take light what may be wrought upon the body of man. . . . We

try also all poisons and other medicines upon them, as well of chirurgery and physic. By art likewise, we make them greater or taller than their kind is; and contrariwise dwarf them, and stay their growth: we make them more fruitful and bearing than their kind is; and contrariwise barren and not generative. Also we make them differ in colour, shape, activity, many ways . . .

Bacon believed fiercely in man's essential preeminence, writing elsewhere: 'Man, if we look to final causes, may be regarded as the centre of the world, insomuch that if man were taken away from the world, the rest would seem to be all astray, without aim or purpose.'

The notion of man at the center of the world, with all else only here to meet our needs, was one that was supported by an all but unchallengeable authority, the Old Testament. If ever a sixteenth-century farmer, preacher or showman needed support for his view that the world of animals (as the world of plants and the rest of the world altogether) was created for himself or his fellows to make use of, he need have looked no further than the first chapter of the first book of the Bible, in which we are told – with biblical conviction – that

God created man in his own image, in the image of God created he him; male and female created he them. And God blessed them, and God said unto them, Be fruitful, and multiply, and replenish the earth, and subdue it: and have dominion over the fish of the sea, and over the fowl of the air, and over every living thing that moveth upon the earth.

Adam is then given the task of naming these animals, and as any postcolonial, poststructuralist or feminist philosopher will tell you, there is no more obvious sign of domination than that.

And Plato and Pythagoras and their metempsychosis theories notwithstanding, the writings of plenty of weighty pre-Christian philosophers were on hand to support this same view of human preeminence.

With meat a staple in all but the poorest diets, with much of the hardest pushing and pulling, lifting and carrying on farms and in towns being done by oxen or horses, and with the second-best and second most popular entertainment available (after the offerings of Jonson, Webster, Shakespeare and Marlowe *inter alia*) being the sight of dogs and bears clawing each other to shreds, most people, perhaps, did not need much convincing.

King James did at least take some interest in the conservation of the lions, if 'conservation' is the right word; under his regime the breeding and rearing of these animals was encouraged, with some success. On 5 August 1604, for instance, it was reported proudly that the lioness called Elizabeth 'whelp'd in the Tow'r'; this event was repeated twice the following year (always the same lioness); and though few of these cubs survived infancy, the births were cause for great celebration at court. James even designed a nipple for a bottle that one fading cub might suckle from. 'I pray God your Lordship can understand my description of a new engine to give a beast suck,' the earl of Montgomery wrote, passing the instructions on to the earl of Salisbury; 'but you must be content to take it as it was delivered unto me.' When the whelp died the king – sentimental as ever – had it 'bowelled and embalmed.'

James was not, of course, particularly concerned with the lions' welfare as such, merely it would seem with trying to ensure that his supplies did not run low.* And before long he had the pleasure of witnessing the slow and dramatic deaths of many of those lions for whose breeding he had been responsible.

And so it was – again – that on 20 April 1610, the king made his way to the Tower to witness the delights of yet another bloody match . . .

This business of baiting lions did not always go quite according to plan. An eighteenth-century guidebook recalled how

> a spaniel dog being once thrown into a former lion's den in the Tower, instead of hurting it, the lion cherished it, and contracted such a fondness for it, that he would never suffer it to be taken out again, but fed it at his table till he died, which was not till several years after.

Both the Dutchman William Schellinks and the Polish aristocrat Teodor Billewicz, visiting after the Restoration, observed the same phenomenon (the latter remarking how striking he found it that the lion was never tempted to eat the dog,

---

* Antonia Fraser has said that James 'took an interest in their feeding arrangements, watching mutton and live chickens being fed to them'; but of course he wasn't interested in anything as benign as animal nutrition, just in good old-fashioned bloodshed.

1. This late-thirteenth-century fresco by Giotto, from the series in the church of San Francesco in Assisi, shows an earnest St Francis in 1215 preaching to the famous flock of birds on the road from Cannara.

2. Two images from the twelfth-century Worksop Bestiary. Certain familiar features identify the first easily as a griffin, depicted with a wild boar, its prey of choice. The second is not quite so obvious, so it is fortunate that the accompanying text is unambiguous; but we can safely assume that before completing the picture the artist never had occasion to see a crocodile in the flesh.

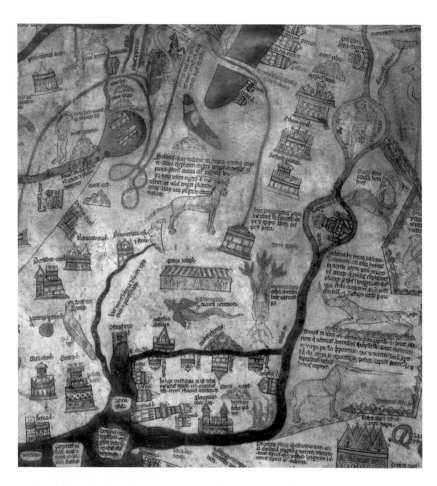

3. Detail from the late-thirteenth-century *Mappa Mundi* at Hereford Cathedral, the only complete wall map of the world known to have survived the Middle Ages, showing a mandrake ('mandragora'), salamander and rhinoceros, among other creatures.

4. *St George and the Dragon* by Paolo Uccello (c. 1460). Medieval art is full of pictures of animals, with dragons and unicorns no less common than animals we see in our zoos today (and depicted with neither more nor less regard for the demands of 'accuracy').

5. 'Le Goût' (taste) from the tapestry sequence known as the *Dame à la Licorne*. The unicorn was not, of course, copied from the life – but neither, we can assume, was the lion. Both have primarily symbolic roles to fulfil (note, for instance, how the faces of the two have been humanized), so whether they are accurate or not is irrelevant.

The Tyger.

Tyger Tyger, burning bright,
In the forests of the night:
What immortal hand or eye,
Could frame thy fearful symmetry?

In what distant deeps or skies,
Burnt the fire of thine eyes?
On what wings dare he aspire?
What the hand, dare sieze the fire?

And what shoulder, & what art,
Could twist the sinews of thy heart?
And when thy heart began to beat,
What dread hand? & what dread feet?

What the hammer? what the chain,
In what furnace was thy brain?
What the anvil? what dread grasp,
Dare its deadly terrors clasp?

When the stars threw down their spears
And water'd heaven with their tears:
Did he smile his work to see?
Did he who made the Lamb make thee?

Tyger Tyger burning bright,
In the forests of the night:
What immortal hand or eye,
Dare frame thy fearful symmetry?

6. 'The Tyger' by William Blake, from his *Songs of Innocence and of Experience*. When Blake came to draw this picture to accompany his famous poem, there were two 'fierce and savage' specimens at the Tower for him to choose from to model for the animal's 'fearful symmetry.'

7. *The Great Indian Rhinoceros* by George Stubbs. Of all the people John Hunter commissioned to paint animals for him, Stubbs was certainly the finest artist. Not only did he capture the appearance of his subjects with unprecedented accuracy (he was a keen anatomist), but his work is also admired for its artistic merit and beauty.

8. The oldest detailed depiction of the Tower, looking west towards London Bridge.
This fifteenth-century illumination appears in the poems of Charles, duke of
Orléans, who was imprisoned in the Tower after the Battle of Agincourt.
By the time of his incarceration the Menagerie had already come to occupy its
long-term site in the southwest corner of the Tower complex.

9. This early fifteenth-century illumination by the Boucicaut Master shows Marco Polo
arriving at the Gulf of Persia from India; the explorer appears to have brought
back with him an array of then entirely unfamiliar animals, in a bid to
impress the people back home. It worked.

10. *John Tradescant the Younger* (1608–62), 'in his Garden,' by Emanuel de Critz. Tradescant and his father kept a Cabinet of Curiosities, which for several decades provided stiff competition to the Menagerie. Much of the collection remains intact today at the Ashmolean Museum in Oxford.

11. John Hunter himself carried out sketches and drawings of many of the animals (alive and dead) in his collection. This *Giraffe* watercolor is believed to be his work.

12. *The Royal College of Surgeons Museum* by T. H. Shepherd (c. 1840). Some years after Hunter's death, his collection – including countless specimens taken from the Tower's animals – was sold to the nation, and became the principal museum of London's Royal College of Surgeons. Though some of the collection succumbed to war damage, much of it is still on permanent display at the College in Lincoln's Inn Fields.

13. *The Monkey Room* by Thomas Rowlandson (1799). This was the one room in the Menagerie where visitors and exhibits were encouraged to mingle freely, occasionally with rather undignified results.

14. *Destruction of the Noble Elephant at Mr Cross's Exeter Exchange.* The tragic death in 1826 of the much-loved Chunee was widely reported in the press, precipitating the publication of numerous handbills and pamphlets, a flurry of outraged letters to the *Times* and even dramatizations of the event for the stage. Awareness was raised not only about the way the animal had been killed, but also the unacceptable conditions in which he and his fellow inmates had been kept.

15. *Extraordinary and Fatal Combat* by Samuel Maunder. This is only one of several depictions of the fight that broke out when a lion and two Bengal tigers were accidentally allowed into the same enclosure on 6 December 1830. The lion died a few days later from the injuries he sustained during his half-hour mauling.

16. For over five centuries the Lion Tower stood at the southwest corner of the Tower site, where the tourist entrance and gift shop can be found today. The foundations on view here beside the entrance are all that is now left to be seen of the Menagerie.

17. The Tower of London today.

'even when he is hungry'). Apparently the lions in question were in no way undiscerning in the matter of which dogs to befriend, however, as a later instance recorded by Gustave Loisel demonstrates:

> A similar phenomenon took place around this time with one of the lions at the Tower of London. When this lion lost the dog he had been living with and befriended, he fell sick. Someone thought it would be a good idea to distract him by throwing other live dogs to him, but he tore them all apart mercilessly.

Much as he enjoyed the spectacle of animals fighting each other, James was not only interested in the Tower animals for provision of entertainment, however; they also gave him a grand opportunity to show off to all sorts of foreign visitors (the kind of people one wants to show off to when one is a king). On one occasion he took the visiting King Christian of Denmark. On another, when James's daughter Elizabeth of Bohemia married Frederick, Elector Palatine, in February 1613, the newlyweds were taken to see the Tower for the bride's father to show off his animals proudly to his new son-in-law. Elizabeth herself must have seen them a hundred times before, and was probably not amused; she entertained herself at the Tower that day by firing one of the cannon instead.

Of all the animals King James owned at various times, in the Menagerie and elsewhere, he had always had a particular fondness – if one may call it that – for the lions. His predecessor on the throne, Elizabeth, though an admirer of animal-baiting,* had a rather more ambivalent relationship with the Menagerie and its animals. She was not fond of the Tower at all (as her mother Anne Boleyn had been beheaded there, and Elizabeth herself imprisoned in the old royal palace building within roaring distance of the animal dens, this is not hard to understand), and had a particular aversion to the Menagerie, whose distracting smells and noises were among the reasons she had decided not to take up permanent residence there as queen. But even she had reason to be grateful to the lions, for making her coronation speech a particularly memorable occasion.

As the story goes, Elizabeth, while unwilling to live in the Tower, agreed to begin her coronation procession from there, just as tradition dictated. So, having spent the previous night in the state apartments in the White Tower, like every monarch before her as far back as Richard II, she was dressed and prepared for her big day, and left the Tower, carried in a richly decorated litter, to begin her great progress through the streets of the capital to Westminster Abbey. After five years shut away fearing for her life, here she was, about to be crowned queen. This was to be a ride in triumph. Outside the Tower gates she stopped to address the assembled crowds, and to pray – aloud – thanking God for her

---

* Animal-baiting, like hunting, was seen primarily as a man's sport, and so it was considered a little peculiar that Her Majesty should take such an interest. A contemporary scribe by the name of Strutt wrote: 'Though a woman, she possessed a masculine mind, and preferred or affected to prefer the exercise of the chase and other recreations pursued by men rather than those usually appropriated to her sex.'

safety: 'O Almighty and Everlasting God,' she began, 'I give Thee most hearty thanks that Thou hast been so merciful unto me to spare me to behold this joyful day. . . .'

The lions, meanwhile, were getting restless; perhaps aware of the great historical significance of what was happening just yards away, on the other side of the wall . . .

'. . . Thou hast dealt as wonderfully and mercifully with me,' she continued, 'as Thou didst with Daniel, whom Thou delivered . . . from the cruelty of the raging lions'; at these words a great growling and roaring was heard just inside the great fortress from which – by the Grace of God – she had just emerged. It is of course possible that in an expert piece of stage-management, Ralph Worsley, royal keeper, had been standing just inside the outer wall, with a marked-up script ('Her Maiesties Coronatioun Speech: Sound Efects') in one hand, and a glowing red-hot poker in the other.

That we will never know. But whatever the actual cause of the animals' outburst, Elizabeth's audience must have been astonished. Such a sign!

One of these lions, as it happens, was later named Elizabeth after the new queen; it was the custom of the day for the reigning monarch to be honored in this way: 'They say that every monarch places one lion there called after their donor, hence one can see a Henry, a Philip, a Mary and an Elizabeth.'*

---

* Visitors must have been entertained by the representative of the living monarch with relics of each of the previous reigns, all gathered together in one place; rather like those oddly satisfying photos of the incumbent president of the United States standing in the Oval Office with all his living predecessors.

It was believed that the health of monarch and lion were mysteriously linked, and that when a monarch fell ill and died, his or her namesake would do the same in solidarity (something of this kind would happen at the death of Charles II). So when, after a forty-five-year reign, the queen fell into her final sickness, the animals' keepers began to cast anxious glances at their elderly charge, who, as it happens, was looking deceptively well. Surprisingly this animal did in fact predecease the queen by a few days, to the relief of all those who had placed trust in the old superstition. Their suspicions were not raised by the fact that as the sixteenth century drew to a close the Menagerie still housed a lion named Edward, after the very-long-dead Edward VI;[*] the treacherous beast, clearly no respecter of tradition, outlived his monarch by almost five decades.

We now know that captive lions do not live anything like this long; we can only assume that in certain cases the death of a lion bearing the name of a living monarch was hushed up (this was not the kind of omen needed by even the most secure king or queen), and the animal quickly replaced by another of the same name. Why they insisted on secretly replacing Edward so long after the death of his namesake king remains a mystery.

Even if these lions did not live prodigiously long lives, however, quite how they survived at all is another mystery. Even with the best will in the world, no one really knew what was required in care of them. Lions and other wildcats were probably best

---

[*] In 1598 the German traveler Paul Hentzner recorded seeing, among other attractions, 'a large lion called Edward VI, from his having been born in that reign.'

off; with their reputation for ferocity (stories of Roman arenas and the like) they were simply given large quantities of meat, which seemed to suit them very well. Trying to second-guess what herbivores would live well on was far harder. For James's collection of live imports from America,* kept in St James's Park, the diet was less satisfactory; the beaver (which must have made it quite clear at once that it was no carnivore) appears to have been given large quantities of bread. Neither the extent of its staying-power nor its comment on the diet afforded it is on record.

A similar fate (whether better or worse is a matter for debate) was in store for James's elephant, which arrived from Spain (with five camels) in 1623, a gift from the Spanish king. Between September and April, said its keepers, this animal would drink nothing but wine, which would, apparently, help to keep out the cold.

And so it was that throughout his short but rather pleasant life this animal was given nothing to drink but wine, a gallon a day. Where the keepers thought elephants would have got access to wine in the wild I don't know, but these beasts are a mystery, and mysteries have notoriously little transaction with logic. Like its thirteenth-century predecessor, we can only assume that this poor, reeling beast did not last long. And when it finally swayed and tottered for the last time, before hitting the ground with a massive crash (which doubtless could be heard all over Christen-

---

* Storks, a beaver ('strange beast as ere any man saw'), cranes, herons — and an American Indian. Yes, alas, an American Indian.

dom), the keepers had no idea why. Had he caught a chill? Maybe they had not given him enough?

Only one man might have rejoiced at the swift demise of this beast; when it was calculated that to keep it would cost upward of £275 a year (*excluding* all the wine), it was remarked that 'The Lord Treasurer will be little in love with presents which cost the King as much to maintain as a garrison.'

Although this was not the first elephant housed in the Tower, the lack of records of how the first had been kept and fed meant that later keepers were unable to learn anything from their predecessors' mistakes. And as late as the end of the eighteenth century elephants were still being given nothing but wine to drink, regardless of the fact that not one elephant had ever survived as long as expected on such a diet. Even after four hundred years of novelty and change, the Menagerie as an institution still had not begun to learn; it was another hundred years before the right questions began to be asked ('How do these animals function?'), and yet another hundred after that before anyone was able to guess at the answers.

Perhaps the greatest threat to the animals' survival around this time was not unwitting mistreatment by their keepers, however, but disease; for after years of relative plaguelessness, London was again experiencing occasional outbreaks. These were of course not of the scale of the Black Death, which had devastated Europe two centuries earlier, but it was bad enough that theatres and other places of public assembly were frequently closed, and many thousands of people died.

Situated on the river bank, inhabitants of the Tower, prisoners and keepers (and animals) alike, were more at threat than most of the capital; every filthy tide that came in brought with it hundreds of rats, which were left scurrying around the cells as the waters receded. The more unfortunate prisoners (human) were kept in those cells down nearest to the river; in 1577 one such prisoner, John Sherwood, described his place of captivity as 'the dongeon amongst the ratts.'

Even Walter Ralegh, who by the standards of the Tower was living in luxury,[*] wrote in 1604 from his cell:

> I am daily in danger of death by the palsy, nightly by
> suffocation by wasted and obstructed lungs. And now the
> plague being come next door to me, and my poor child
> having laid this fortnight next door to a woman with a
> running plague sore and but a paper wall between them –
> and her child is, this Thursday, dead of the plague.

But somehow the royal animals, underfed and subject to ill treatment and disease, seemed to thrive, and the public – the nobility, local merchants, foreign tourists or traders or ambassadors – continued to flock to the Tower to see them. When Frederick, the duke of Württemberg, visited London in 1592, his secretary recorded seeing small wooden houses containing a lion and lioness, both (we are told admiringly) over a hundred years old. The rumor of these animals' longevity was spread widely and

---

[*] And not just compared to Sherwood and the royal animals; at one point Robert
Cecil wrote that Ralegh was 'lodged and attended as well in the Tower as in his
house.'

believed absolutely. When the Swiss chemist Thomas Platter visited London in 1599, a tour in which his visit to the Tower featured as one of the highlights, he recorded the same detail in his journal:

> We likewise saw six lions and lionesses in this stronghold, in separate cages and two were over 100 years old. And if I remember one was named Edward, and one of the lionesses, Elisabeth. Not far from them was a lean, ugly wolf, the only one in England, it is true, kept for this reason by the queen, as there is not another in the whole realm, except for a number in Scotland, which kingdom is only distinct and divided from England by a river.
>
> Quite close to them were also a tiger and a porcupine. And but for a little a lion might have caught one of the party's servants, for it could get its claws through the bars of the cage in which they fed.

There were royal and private zoos scattered all across Europe at the start of the seventeenth century – among the better known were at Florence (where there were three), Prague (with a large number of camels at this time for some reason), Philip IV of Spain's Casa del Campo, Dresden, Ghent and Sicily. A well-traveled man like Platter would doubtless have seen others on his travels – perhaps he visited the collection at Ebersdorf, just a couple of hundred miles from his hometown of Basel – so it is revealing that the Tower collection managed to impress him.

Platter was not alone among London's foreign visitors in finding the lions (perennial favorites) and other beasts a worthwhile draw in the capital. Around the same time Paul Hentzner saw 'three lionesses, one Lion of great size . . . a Tyger, a Lynx; a Wolf . . . Porqupine, and an Eagle . . . kept in a remote place, fitted up for the purpose with lattices at the Queen's expense.' It is unfortunate, incidentally, that around this time it is only the foreign visitors who bothered to record their visits; although we know that many Londoners did frequent the Menagerie in the time of Elizabeth and James, it is not until the days of Pepys and Evelyn that we have anecdotal records of such visits. Nor do we know how much people paid for admission, though it was unlikely to have been a fixed rate (at least one visitor commented on the arbitrariness of it and complained that he had been charged far too high a price). A sensible guess would be something in the region of 3d (at a time when the average weekly wage was 12d, a ticket to stand and hear a play at the far less exclusive Globe Theatre a penny). But although this would put the Menagerie extremely high on the price-scale for public entertainment, there always seemed to be someone prepared to pay whatever was required for the experience of seeing live lions and wolves – probably for the first time.

But greater than any foreign tourist, the Menagerie's most constant supporter was King James himself. In 1622, three years before his death, he had improvements made to his (still relatively recent) viewing platform over the yard; the new structure was to be almost 98 feet long and would have a very secure handrail (extremely important). From this new vantage point, James could watch one of his newer favorites, a tiger that had been pre-sented in 1613 by the ambassador extraordinary of Savoy. When this animal arrived on 1 July (along with a lioness and the remains of 'a lynx which died on the road'), he joined a distinguished company, including eleven lions, two leopards, three eagles, two mountain cats and a jackal. There were also other royal tigers in London at this time, housed on Bankside at the Paris Garden, a public park (and home to a small but eclectic collection including several crocodiles and a Virginian flying squirrel), but it is an indication of James's attachment to this one in particular that he chose it to be kept with his other prized possessions at the Tower, where he could easily visit it and watch it eating, at play or in fight.

Unlike his father, Prince Charles (younger brother to the now deceased Prince of Wales) took no great interest in the animals in the Tower. It was this prince, as Charles I, who ordered the construction at Whitehall of Inigo Jones's Cockpit-in-Court, a theater-cum-cockpit; common cockfighting and plays were more to the new king's taste than the supposedly refined sport of lion-baiting. There is only one account of Charles attending a baiting (in 1637), and this did not even take place at the Tower; but the Menagerie survived the king's relative neglect with great ease. And it was not long before the ill-fated Charles was beheaded; it was said that when he died all the spaniels in the country wept at the loss. Charles was almost certainly not much missed among the neglected Menagerie staff, except perhaps by the keeper Samuel Cordwell, who through no fault of his own lost his job as part of the new order.*

---

* This allowed the position to revert back to the faithful Gill family, who shortly thereafter completed a century in office, a record that had been interrupted only by Cordwell's few years' tenure under the unfortunate and divisive Charles.

The unappreciative (and certainly underappreciated) Charles was replaced by a far greater threat to the Menagerie's future; this new danger, an *active* threat, had begun to loom large throughout the 1640s, in the shape of Oliver Cromwell, his Council of State and his furious programs of reform and moral improvement.

By the beginning of the Commonwealth in 1649 (following Charles's execution at the Banqueting House), steps had been taken to outlaw – or, better still, to ban outright – the baiting of animals in the capital. Cromwell himself went to great lengths to impose such a ban, simultaneously with his bans on theatrical performances and the like. The first decree had been made in 1642, with the doomed King Charles still nominally in charge; the second was a direct edict from the Council of State, in 1653, some years after his removal from the scene. Cromwell chose Colonel Thomas Pride, responsible for the famous purge of Presbyterians from Parliament in 1648 (and a year later signatory to the king's death warrant), to enforce this decree. On 9 February 1655, Pride arrived at Bear Gardens, Henslowe's Hope, to put an end to the cruel sport of bear-baiting once and for all.

But the reforming zeal of the Council of State was clearly not an attempt to curb the cruelty being inflicted on animals (that is a notion still some years off). After all, does it seem likely that animal welfare was foremost in Pride's mind when he and his company of soldiers arrived at the Hope and he insisted on personally putting all the animals to death 'with his own hand'? Rather the Council's order was merely an attempt to limit the excesses of (sinful) humanity, in just the same way that the puritanical city fathers had tried to close the theatres and bearpits half a century earlier.

In this case, however, it was not mere pleasure that the Puritans objected to (though, as God was their witness, the audiences *were* having a great deal of fun) so much as the fact that this kind of entertainment was particularly distasteful because it brought out the brutal (animal) side of its human spectators – leading to betting, drinking, swearing, indulging in morally indefensible conduct with members of the opposite sex, and so on.

Besides this, writes the historian Keith Thomas,

> because the mutual ferocity of wild animals was a response to Man's sin, all animals having been tame until the Fall, it followed that it was wrong for men to take pleasure in watching fights between them . . . Puritans lamented the readiness of dogs to fight with bears because they saw it as the result of the Fall and therefore a reminder of Man's sin.

Whatever the motivation, the powerful interregnum government did meet with some limited success in this enterprise; baiting did indeed stop in the Tower, though this was probably as much a factor of not having a champion (and sponsor) as it had had in the good old days of King James. And sports of this kind did decrease in frequency and popularity throughout the city during this period, though they were not fully eliminated from the entertainment life of the capital (and criminalized) for some time. Cock-fighting was the last such sport to be banned (hunting excepted)* and survived until as late as 1849.

---

* Hunting is being debated, apparently endlessly, to this day.

In other ways – ways less offensive to Cromwell and his Council – the Menagerie was flourishing. In 1657, writing his extravagantly overtitled *Londinopolis: An Historicall Discourse or Perlustration of the City of London, the Imperial Chamber, and Chief Emporium of Great Britain*, James Howell described the history of the Menagerie, adding, 'Nor was the Tower ever better furnish'd with Lions than it is now, there being six in all, both young and old.' And it remained as popular with the public as ever. When the Pole Sebastian Gawarecki visited during the years of the Commonwealth, he saw a healthy-looking collection of beasts including not just the lions ('very big beasts'), but also tigers, lynxes, an 'Indian cat from Virginia' (possibly a puma), and 'a skin of a snake killed in the Thames some time ago.'

Samuel Pepys, the celebrated diarist of the 1660s, was another frequent visitor. The first visit recorded in his brand-new diary took place on 11 January 1660 (just ten days after his first entry). Although Pepys could not have known it, this was just months before the collapse of the interregnum government, and the restoration of the monarchy in the person of the soon-to-be Charles II, whose boat came in to Dover on 25 May, bringing the new king home from his eleven years in exile.

5
Going to See the Lions

To dinner to my Lady Sandwich; and Sir Tho. Crewes children coming thither, I took them and all my Lady's to the Tower and showed them the lions and all that was to be shown, and so took them to my house and made much of them; and so saw them back to my Lady's – Sir Th. Crewes children being as pretty and the best behaved that ever I saw of their age.

—Samuel Pepys, *Diary*, 3 May 1662

This description by Pepys is only one of several accounts in his *Diary* of visits to the lions in the Tower. What makes this unusual and surprising is not that he and the children appear to have had a good time – weren't hundreds of people having fun visiting the Tower every day of the week? – but that he had thought to take the children there in the first place. Not because he might have feared alarming them, or losing them in the crowds, but just because at that time the predominant view was still that children were lesser, inadequate beings and not worth trying to amuse. Surely it would be a waste of money? It would be years before the birth of the new sensibilities that would see childhood as a significant and formative stage. With the exception of royal children, Pepys's visit in 1662 marks the earliest record of children being taken to see the lions, and by a considerable margin.

This entirely new conception of childhood, the idea that 'the child is father to the man,' is a Romantic notion, and as such a century and more away (the line itself 'the child is father to the man' comes originally from the Romantic poet William Wordsworth). Compare this to Milton, for instance, writing *Paradise Regained* in the same decade as Pepys's visit to the Tower with the Crewes and Sandwich children: 'The childhood shews the man, as morning shews the day.' Milton is quite advanced on the subject, and does at least acknowledge the link between boy and man, but not the ways in which the experiences of one can actually *cause* the condition of the other. Childhood doesn't affect or alter age, it is simply identical in nature to it, reflecting it, predicting it. So, frankly, after all this the idea that one should have consideration for *animals*, and concern for the effects of the way in which dumb beasts are treated, is utterly ludicrous . . .

Pepys himself was a great fan of the Menagerie in the Tower. In one of the first entries in his diary he had described stopping by there on his way from an alehouse at Covent Garden to his home at Axe Yard in Westminster, to see his favorite animal, an old lion by the name of Crowly: 'I went towards London and in my way went in to see Crowly, who was now grown a very great lion and very tame' (*Diary*, 11 January 1660).

Anyone familiar with the layout of the city of London, then as now, will know that Pepys, far from stopping by 'on the way,' must have taken a considerable detour, more than doubling his journey home, in order to pay this friendly call. Quite a sign of devotion in the bitter January weather.

Some years later, in the mid-1670s, sadly not within the scope of the *Diary*, Pepys was himself sent a lion cub by a Mr Martin, then the British consul at Algiers. This animal came to be lodged at Derby House in Westminster, where the Admiralty was based and where Pepys himself now lived (it is probably for the best that the houseproud Mrs P. was long dead by now), and according to Pepys the beast was more than comfortable there; a letter to Martin described Pepys's new friend as 'as tame as you sent him and as good company.' It is an endearing thought that Pepys might have remembered his old friend Crowly (now doubtless dead) as he welcomed Mr Martin's gift into the Pepys family circle. Pepys's biographer, Claire Tomalin, has suggested that when Pepys himself was sent to the Tower in 1679, he might have moved this animal in with the royal collection there, so it could board close to its master.

Pepys does attempt a third visit to the Menagerie in the years covered by the *Diary*, but is thwarted by the inexplicable (to him) lack of curiosity of Will Stankes, his father's old bailiff:

> but Lord, what stir Stankes makes with his being crowded in the streets and wearied in walking in London, and would not be woo'd by my wife and Ashwell to go to a play nor to Whitehall or to see the Lyons, though he was carried in a coach. I never could have thought there had been upon earth a man so little curious in the world as he is.
>
> —*Diary*, 30 April 1663

On his way home from his visits to Crowly in the Tower, Pepys would almost certainly have walked down Eastcheap, passing what is now the site of the monument marking the Great Fire, which would soon sweep through the city. On Sunday, 2 September 1666, Pepys and his wife were to be awakened by a servant 'to tell us of a great fire they saw in the City.' And that evening he stood on the Bankside and with tears in his eyes watched his beloved London burning to the ground.

After a ten-month drought the houses of London burned all too easily, and the fire spread quickly eastwards, towards Tower Hill. The Tower had been thought unbroachable, even by fire, and it was here that London's goldsmiths had thought to leave their jewelery and money for safe-keeping. These valuables were no mere trifles; the whole hoard was valued at an unimaginable £1.2 million. And this was not all that was at stake. The Tower was also packed with supplies belonging to His Majesty's Navy, among them large quantities of gunpowder.

And of course the western entrance, the wing of the Tower closest to the flames, was full of animals too. It was said that as the fire approached, the panicked animals began to roar and shriek and throw themselves against the bars of their cages. In the general distress and panic no thought was given to the animals, no attempt made to move them; not surprising, perhaps, given the demands on the attention by the threat to the money, the gold and the gunpowder. Besides, if the fire were allowed to reach the gunpowder, it would have done the animals no good at all.

As John Evelyn wrote in his diary that day, if the fire had reached the White Tower and the magazine there, it 'would undoubtedly have not onely beaten downe & destroyed all the bridge, but sunke &

torne all the vessells in the river, & rendred the demolition beyond all expression for severall miles.'

Rumors quickly spread that the explosions in the vicinity of the Tower were being caused by the firing of the cannon there, which, it was said, were being used to clear the area of all contiguous buildings. Even without resorting to the cannon many buildings in the path of the fire were pulled down. Pepys himself helped with this. But however fast the buildings were torn down, the fire continued to encroach eastwards, and panic spread eastwards with it.

An account written a few weeks after the fire was brought under control described how on the Tuesday 'as though frightened by the stronghold of the Tower, the fire stopped beneath its walls.' Perhaps it was not the fire's cowering at the prospect of the Tower that brought it under control, but the good fortune of a change in wind; this was an easterly wind, at last, and before long it became clear that the Tower was safe, to the great relief of Londoners. And it was not just a matter of gold and gunpowder; for symbolic reasons too it was significant that it was still standing strong, undefeated.* And the Menagerie too continued to draw visitors, even with the city to its west devastated by the blaze. The Tower, some six hundred years old, was a great symbol of strength and continuity (it had survived the breaching by the Peasants' Revolt, invasions, revolutions, coups and worse), and the Menagerie the part of it for which Londoners felt the greatest affection. They certainly felt many

---

* The danger to the Tower was never again to be underestimated. Later that same year the lieutenant of the Tower, Sir John Robinson, ordered the purchase of three hundred buckets and ten ladders, as well as engines, hooks, et cetera, for storage at the Tower. Just in case.

things for the Tower itself – awe, fear, respect – but never 'affection' or anything like it.

Old bailiff Stankes was in a tiny minority unimpressed by the spectacles of the Menagerie. On the whole the people of London were proud of this attraction in the heart of their city, an attraction unrivaled in the country; and they expressed their pride by frequent visits, and by exhortations to their out-of-town visitors to follow their example. In particular it was the presence of lions – adopted British lions – in the city that was a matter of the greatest pride (sorry). After the Restoration the number of recreational visitors to the Tower, Londoners and tourists, had soared, making it by far the most popular tourist attraction in the capital. Had there still been restrictions on who was allowed to visit, Pepys would have got in on the strength of his post as a public official, but in fact it's likely that around now the collections in the Tower became truly public. If you had the admission fee you were welcome. And visitors to the Tower in the second half of the century could see not only the Menagerie but the Royal Armouries too; and from the mid-1660s they had even been allowed to catch a glimpse of the spectacular Crown Jewels, many of them lately created for Charles's coronation,* and all newly put on display for an awestruck public (many of them still on view today). Pepys described his first sighting of these treasures, on 23 April 1668:

> After dinner carried them [his guests] to the Tower and
> showed them all to be seen there; and among other things,

---

* The old set had been melted down during the recent troubles.

the Crown and Scepters and rich plate, which I myself
never saw before and endeed is noble – and I mightily
pleased with it.*

It is likely that this display of the Crown Jewels and other of the
Tower's trappings had less to do with a desire to impress (as the
animals had long been) than a fairly bold gesture of populariz-
ation – making the king's treasures the people's treasures, an
acknowledgment, perhaps, that (like his unfortunate father)
Charles had come to recognize that he was answerable to his
people. The new king comes home from his time in exile and
throws open the doors . . .

Colonel Blood's attempt to steal these royal jewels in 1671
was clearly too literal an interpretation of this idea for the king's
liking. The king pardoned him, however, and then quite inexplicably gave him a piece of property in Ireland and a very generous
pension. But had he been imprisoned in the Tower, as surely he
must have expected, Blood would at least have found himself in
good company. The reigns of Charles II and James II would see
some extremely distinguished Tower residents (willing and not so
willing), among them the vicious Judge Jeffreys, William Penn (of
Pennsylvania fame), the Popish plotter Titus Oates and even
Samuel Pepys himself. Later, during the reigns of William and
Mary and of Queen Anne, prisoners tended to be miscellaneous

---

* Among this party Pepys brought to the Tower to show off the lions and such was
Elizabeth Knepp, with whom he was carrying on a sort of affair. The illicit
couple then left the others and went on to Vauxhall ('Fox-Hall'), 'And there she
and I drank; and yo did tocar her corps and besar sans fin her.'

rebels from miscellaneous rebellious plots, usually trying to replace the newly secure Protestant succession with the exiled James II (as he later became) or one of his equally undesirable Catholic allies.

Politically there was constant insecurity of one kind or another throughout the reign of Charles II, constant anxiety about the stability of the monarch, and indeed of the monarchy. So much so that when a trio of Tower lions died in 1681 it was felt that some gesture of reassurance was in order, to indicate that Charles the Lion was still alive and well. So appeared the 'Lion's Elegy' ('Verses on the death of three lions in the Tower'):

> Three Lions dead! O strange! O strange! What then?
> And must not Lions dye as well as Men?
> But 'tis prodigious, and hence some Divine,
> That Monarchy will fall, or else decline.
> That we once more shall be without a King.
> And in his Room a Common-Wealth shall spring,
> Let not such Thoughts trouble a wise Man's Head,
> The Lion, Charles the second, is not dead . . .
>
> —Anonymous

Charles's predecessors – especially his grandfather James – had all been the victims of odd animal gifts from foreign monarchs, and Charles himself was no different. Among those he received was an Arab horse that was presented to him by the Russian ambassador in 1662. Although this animal may not have found a home in the Tower (St James's Park was still a convenient alternative, as it had been in James's day), the Tower could boast an excellent set of lions, among them Pepys's friend Crowly, and the lions' canine companion. And the collection was always growing (or at least always changing). By the time John Strype produced his new edition of Stow's *Survey* in 1704, the Menagerie was said to contain:

Six LIONS. First, a She Lion; which was presented to King *William* by Admiral *Russel*. Secondly, a He Lion, being about Six Years old; brought over by Captain *Littleton*. Sir *Thomas Littleton* presented him to King *William*. Thirdly, Another Lion presented to Queen *Anne* by the Lord *Grandville*: it came to the *Tower* on *Easter-Monday*, *Anno* 1703. Fourthly, Two young Lions, sent to Queen *Anne* from the King of *Barbary*. They came in *October*, 1703. Fifthly, Yet another young Lion, brought over for the young Duke of *Glocester*.

Two LEOPARDS, or Tygers. One ever since K. *Charles* the Second's Time; but now in Decay: the other very beautiful and lovely to look upon; lying and playing, and turning upon her Back wantonly, when I saw her.

Three EAGLES, in several Apartments. One had been there Fourteen or Fifteen Years; called a *Bald Eagle*, with a white Head and Neck.

Two *Swedish* OWLS, of a great Bigness, called *Hopkins*. They were presented to K. *Charles*.

CATS of the Mountains, Two: Walking continually backwards and forwards. One of them was presented to Queen *Anne*; of the colour somewhat of a Hare: much larger than our ordinary domestick Cats; and very cruel.

A JACKALL. Much like a Fox, but bigger, and longer legged, and more grisled.

These Creatures have a rank Smell; which hath so affected the Air of the Place, (tho' there is a Garden adjoining) that it hath much injured the Health of the Man that attends them, and so stuffed up his Head, that it affects his Speech. And yet their Dens are cleansed every Day; and they have fresh Water set them every Day and Night.

Here be also the Skins of Two dead Lions stuffed. One died two Days before K. *Charles* the Second.

The Tower's popularity, and consequent potential as a royal money-spinner, did not go unnoticed by those in charge, and in 1672 a wide-ranging program of investment in the Menagerie began, the most ambitious change it had seen in over half a century. The plans for reform and expansion were under the care of the surveyor-general of the King's Works, then none other than the young man – 'that miracle of a Youth,' as his friend John Evelyn called him – Christopher (soon to be Sir Christopher) Wren. Wren had been given this post (one formerly occupied by the great architect and draftsman Inigo Jones) in March 1669; as surveyor-general he was chief architect to the Crown, the member of the Royal Household responsible for the planning, building and maintaining of most of the king's grandest properties: not the Tower as a rule (general maintenance for which fell in theory within the portfolio of the Office of Ordnance), but the Palace at Whitehall, Hampton Court, St James's, Greenwich and several others. For this he received the handsome wage of £28 8s 4d per month (purchasing power of $5,500 today), plus a house in Scotland Yard, 'riding charges' and numerous perks.

In July 1671 Wren signed a contract to build a new house for the keeper, Robert Gill. Work began a year later on the Lion House, a custom-built two-story keeper's residence in the southeast corner of the Lion Tower. By the time it was completed in 1675 the keepership had been passed on to William Gill, the last of the Essex-born family to occupy the post; the first of the line, Thomas Gill, had been appointed in 1573, a century earlier.

Perhaps the most extraordinary and important result of this process of development had nothing in fact to do with the structure or workings of the Menagerie itself, but came to light quite by accident on 17 July 1674, during Wren's preliminary excavations. He had been told to start by clearing the White Tower 'of all contiguous buildings.' This proved to be a more significant job than either Wren or the king had anticipated.

In his tribute-volume *Parentalia*, Wren's son described how his illustrious father 'was rebuilding some Parts of the Tower of London,' when to the surprise of his men 'the Bones of King Edward the 4th Children . . . were, after 191 years, found.' The great man had, it appeared, stumbled upon the bones of the young King Edward V and his brother Richard, Duke of York, the two royal boys commonly known as the 'Princes in the Tower.' The bones had been found 'about ten feet deep in the Ground, in a wooden Chest, as the Workmen were taking away the Stairs, which led from the royal Lodgings into the Chapel of the White Tower.'

King Charles was told at once of this discovery, and without hesitation ordered that the bones be transferred to Westminster Abbey to be given the proper burial they had been denied two centuries earlier. It could only do Charles's image good to uphold the symbolic importance of the rites and rights of monarchy, of tradition and respect. After his father's unhappy fate, the new king knew all too well how much was at stake.

But in fact the bones lay in the Tower for four years, and it was not until 1678 that a quiet ceremony was finally held in the Abbey to bury the princes' remains in a white marble urn designed by Wren himself. But what neither the king nor those officiating at the service knew was that the final laying to rest of the princes was incomplete – they were only burying a partial set of bones. They had, after all, been left lying around unguarded for all this time since being uncovered, and by now quite a number of them had been removed mysteriously and replaced with animal bones. (According to Sir George Buck, there had been an earlier occasion, at the start of the century, when a man called John Webb believed he had discovered the princes' bones; but these turned out to be those of a long-dead Menagerie ape.)

In a second phase of work just a few years later, Wren supervised the construction of a set of new cages for James I's old exercise yard, to house a number of large birds and a 'Jana' (a hyena?). Around this time it was said that, in the Tower, 'they show crowns and sceptres, axes and clubs, lions, leopards and other terrible things.' But by now such 'terrible things' – and not just animals – could be seen in a dozen other places in London too, not just at the Tower; which competition could yet prove a problem for the Gills and their fellow keepers.

Even by the start of the seventeenth century London had

become known as a place where a man could make his fortune if he could find something sufficiently freakish to put on public exhibition. When Shakespeare came to write *The Tempest* around 1611, he had his jester Trinculo stumble upon the monster Caliban (a strange creature – 'a man or a fish?' he wonders), and say:

> Were I in England now, as once I was, and but had this fish painted, not a holiday fool there but would give a piece of silver; there would this monster make a man; any beast there makes a man. When they will not give a doit to relieve a lame beggar, they will lay out ten to see a dead Indian.

Besides the more established and respectable collections, not just the British Museum but the panoramas and dioramas and the like, there were always strange temporary apparitions, whether the amazing self-exhibited fat man Daniel Lambert, who at his death weighed a magnificent 53 stone – 742 pounds – or Van Butchell's tasteful exhibition of the body of his lately embalmed wife (a display not much approved of by the second Mrs Van Butchell, for obvious reasons).

Most of the sights that were considered worth seeing in the capital, even the relatively respectable ones, were far newer attractions than the Tower – and even those few of comparable age were only now for the first time seeing surges in visitor numbers, like the Tower itself. The very first among the new permanent shows was the 'Ark,' the collection of curiosities assembled by the John Tradescants, father and son, that has the distinction of having been the very first museum in Britain. One

German visitor, Georg Christoph Stirn, arriving in London in the summer of 1638, went first to the Tower Menagerie and then to the Ark, and declared then that he'd seen everything this city had to offer and was quite ready to go home now if that'd be all right . . .

And though he did return to Nürnberg rather poorer for not having seen Westminster Abbey or Old St Paul's Cathedral (the great old building doomed to stand for just twenty-eight more years), Stirn was certainly right in his assessment that the Tradescants' collection was an excellent complement to the Menagerie's. In many ways the weaknesses of one were matched by the strengths of the other. At the heart of the Tradescants' displays were their botanical samples, assembled in their traveling years; but besides them the Ark also showed an unparalleled collection of 'rarities': dodos, unicorn horns and the like. In 1625 John Tradescant the Elder had written to the secretary of the Navy asking that he spread the word that he would be interested in acquiring 'Anything that is Strange.' In his *Travels* Peter Mundy wrote of the Ark that 'a Man might in one daye behold and collecte into one place more Curiosities than hee should see if hee spend all his life in Travell.'

There was some attempt to assemble comparable nonliving displays in the Tower, also described in Mundy's *Travels*, and Tradescant reported having seen them there too. Apparently there was even a unicorn horn there. What is more, when the duke of Stettin-Pomerania had paid his visit to the Tower in the early years of the century, he saw not only what he took to be a unicorn's horn, but also a gown lined with unicorn fur. How could any visitor fail to be seduced by such a display?

John Tradescant the Elder had spent years in the service of Robert Cecil, the first earl of Salisbury, creating a spectacularly ambitious garden for him at Hatfield House. This project had led Tradescant out of the country on shopping excursions – expenses paid by the earl, of course – to find new botanical species to grace his magnificent creation. The autumn of 1611 saw him traveling all through the Netherlands, Belgium and France – by the time he returned to England at the very end of December, he had collected over a thousand specimens. His time at Hatfield in the service of the earl (and then his son the second earl) was followed by a time in Canterbury and employment by George Villiers, duke of Buckingham, who was, after the king, the most powerful man in the country. Before his death in 1638 Tradescant had also worked for the king himself, and in his last year would be appointed first keeper of the Botanic Gardens in Oxford, the first of its kind in the country. He had traveled all over Europe and to the New World, and many of the specimens he and his son John assembled – some of the first generation of North American exotica – graced the gardens of the great and the good of seventeenth-century England, while others were put on public display in the family 'Ark.'

Tradescant's first stop in Paris would almost certainly have been to call on the great botanist and collector Jean Robin. Robin had masterminded the recently opened Jardin des Plantes (then still called the Jardin du Roi), the botanical gardens just to the southeast of the city, built for the provision of plant products for the medical school (it was later opened to the public, but not until 1635). Robin, an admirer of Tradescant, was delighted to see him; he sold his English guest fig and pomegranate trees, and gave him numerous others to take back to Hatfield with him.

Walking the Jardin des Plantes today, within the sound of traffic from rue de Buffon, rue Cuvier and the Gare d'Austerlitz, there is surprisingly little that is changed since the days of Tradescant's visit. The grid layout of the central garden is just the same, though the surrounding buildings have been replaced; and there is even one tree still alive and well that Tradescant would have known. One of Robin's most prized acquisitions, a 'faux acacia' had been grown from a cutting sent to him some years earlier from London, probably by Tradescant himself, who had just received a delivery of strange and exciting things from Virginia. The tree is still there, and today's guidebooks boast of it as 'the oldest tree in Paris.'*

If a contemporary of Tradescant's, visiting the Jardin des Plantes, had turned towards the northeastern corner of the park, his back towards Robin's promising sapling, he would have seen no more than a small scattering of cages, housing a handful of animals, the embryonic Paris Menagerie. In 1611 it was certainly nothing to write home about, and so, sadly, Tradescant didn't bother. He was after all a Londoner, and knew the Tower's spectacular collection too well to be impressed by some half-hearted foreign effort. Nor did any of the other English travelers

---

* The tree is now called *Robinia pseudacacia*, 'Robin's false acacia'; this was not the last time Tradescant missed out on bequeathing his name to his discoveries or creations for posterity (this would be the fate of his museum).

of the period bother to record their visits in their letters home, if indeed they thought it worth visiting at all.

This same corner still houses the remains – struggling along, now rather shabby and largely ignored – of Paris's once great Menagerie. Today it is a sad and lonely place, where forgotten animals pace up and down cramped and dirty enclosures, and no one much takes any notice. At the height of its popularity it was to prove influential in the demise of the Menagerie in the Tower of London; but back at the start of the seventeenth century it was still no more than an experiment, no competition for the already thriving animal collections elsewhere on the continent.

And there were a lot of them. Britain was not the only country engaged in forming links to Asia and the Americas through exploration and trade, links that were spreading ever faster, and that brought these odd animal souvenirs as a sort of measure of their scope. It's hardly surprising, then, that by the mid–seventeenth century every country in Europe boasted collections like this – some, like Italy and France, had several. During his European travels in 1644–45, Pepys's near-contemporary and fellow diarist John Evelyn visited menageries at Rome, Padua, Florence and Paris. And there were literally dozens of others, from Prague to Brussels. Florence's *seraglio delle fiere*, perhaps the best stocked, Evelyn found far superior to the Tower. It is, he says,

> a place where are kept several wild beasts, as wolves, cats, bears, tigers and lions. They are loose in a deep-welled court, and therefore to be seen with more pleasure than those at the Tower of London, in their grates. One of the

A True and Perfect Description

OF

The Strange and VVonderful

ELEPHANT

Sent from the

East - Indies .

And brought to *London* on *Tuesday* the Third
of *August* , 1 6 7 5.

With a Discourse of the Nature and Qualities of Elephants in General.

With Allowance.

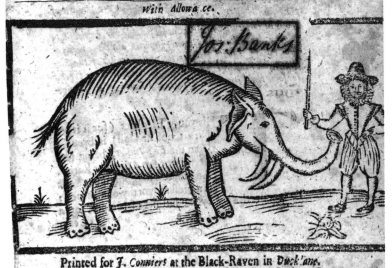

Jos: Banks

Printed for *J. Conniers* at the Black-Raven in *Duck-lane.*

One of many pamphlets describing the exotic animals brought to London
from the East; this specimen (the pamphlet, that is) clearly once belonged
to the botanist Joseph Banks.

lions leaped to a surprising height, to catch a joint of mutton which I caused to be hung down.

—*Diary*, 25 October 1644

Paris's comparatively small collection by the Tuileries gardens, which Evelyn visited on 9 February 1644, was also marked by having not just 'a building in which are kept for the King's pleasure, a bear, a wolf, a wild boar, a leopard, &c.' but also 'noble hedges of pomegranates, fountains, fish-ponds, and an aviary.'

By the second half of the century, incidentally, such collections in France had acquired the name *ménagerie*. The word for 'housekeeping' (*ménage*) had developed into *ménagerie*, referring to agricultural management in general, and then specifically the place where animals were kept captive. The word would transfer to England by the beginning of the next century, very soon afterwards to be used with reference to the Tower collection.

Evelyn's relative dislike of the Tower's animal collection did not stop him from visiting it on occasion, however, or from keeping abreast of its news and acquisitions. In 1682 he records in his diary a gift to King Charles from the Moroccan ambassador, of 'Lions & Estridges.' According to Sir John Reresby, the king was not enormously impressed: 'That embassadours present to the King was two lyons and thirty ostiges, which His Majesty laughed at, saying he knew nothing fitter to return for them than a flock of geese.'

However, His Majesty did allow the two lions to join their fellows in the Tower. The thirty ostriches really didn't appeal, though, and they were moved to join the other birds in St James's Park, in the collection that had till lately included a couple of pelicans (from Astrakhan, on the Caspian Sea), described by Evelyn as looking 'very melancholy.'* The ostriches didn't stay in the Park long; they were soon given away – to any courtier who'd have them.

Although Evelyn himself did not think much of the Tower, he could never be said to represent popular tastes (for one thing he thought baiting 'barbarous,' quite unaccountably). Whatever Evelyn's thoughts, the Tower was undeniably popular with most of his fellow Londoners. His *Diary* is full of colorful characters (friends like Pepys and Christopher Wren, acquaintances like the master carver Grinling Gibbons and the royal astronomer John Flamsteed, the latter based at the Tower), most of them better attuned to the tastes of the times, and admirers of the Menagerie. Evelyn does at least show some interest in Tradescant's Ark, and records a meeting with Elias Ashmole, the man the collection would be passed on to after the death of Tradescant the Younger (after a certain amount of legal wrangling with the widowed Mrs Tradescant). It is with the somewhat shady Ashmole, and not the Tradescants, that the Ark collection is now most associated, in fact; it was subsequently moved to Oxford where it survives today under his name, as the Ashmolean Museum.

---

* Birdcage Walk, which runs along the south side of the park, was named for this collection; the birds' keeper, Edward Storey, gave his name in turn to the adjoining Storey's Gate.

*

Looking a little way into the future, we can see that the acquisitive Ashmole was not to be content with the collection left him at Tradescant's death, and supplemented it with all sorts of curiosities obtained by equally questionable means. By the 1670s, Tradescant's old collection had acquired the lantern used by Guy Fawkes to light his way into the bowels of Parliament, Oliver Cromwell's death mask, a shell-studded mantle belonging to Powhattan, father to the American Indian princess Pocahontas,[*] the surviving pieces of Tradescant's dodo,[†] and even a handful of the mysteriously disappeared bones of the 'Princes in the Tower.' Apart from the princes' bones, which vanished in the early eighteenth century, all these curiosities are still on view at the

---

[*] Pocahontas, the English-speaking princess from the New World, was brought over to England, with her husband John Rolfe, in 1616. As recorded in Ben Jonson's *Staple of News*, she was given lodgings at the Belle Sauvage inn at Ludgate (the inn's name is merely a coincidence, and predates her arrival by a century or so) and quickly became something of an attraction herself. During her short time in England she was much feted and examined: she was taken to the Tower to meet the imprisoned Sir Walter Ralegh, she was invited to court masques (on Twelfth Night, 1617) and had her portrait painted, and became the New World's first convert to Christianity. She died in 1617 of smallpox.

[†] This exhibit had not lasted well. A statute of the Ashmolean stated that should a display begin to grow 'old and perishing,' it should be eliminated and a newer replacement for it found. Legend has it that in 1755 an order was given for the dodo (which was admittedly growing more than a little mangy) to be burnt, before it occurred to anyone that replacing it might be a little awkward, seeing as they don't make them anymore, what with extinction and all. . . . A few bits of unburnt dodo (skull, foot) were rescued just in time, and are still on show.

Ashmolean Museum (not, please note, the Tradescantean Museum) in Oxford today.*

Even without these additions, however, the Tradescants' collection in Lambeth was already very popular, and by now it was by no means unique. Not only were there numerous menageries all over Europe, but by this time the Tower even faced a considerable amount of competition at home. Back in December 1635, keeper Robert Gill had issued a petition against one Thomas Ward:

> His late Majesty by his letters patent dated 21st July, in the 10th year of his reign, guaranteed that thenceforth no person should at any time carry any lion or leopard into any part of England to shew them for gain, upon such forfeiture as by any laws may be inflicted on them. Notwithstanding, Thomas Ward, although he has been warned and also prohibited by the Vice-Chancellor of Oxford and Cambridge, has gone about the country with a lion both at the Act at Oxford and at Sturbridge Fair in Cambridge, and other places to shew it for money, and since has parted with it to Martin Brocas and John Watson, who in like manner carry the same about, notwithstanding [the lion] has grown so fierce that he almost killed a little child, and bit his keeper so that he lay eight weeks of the sore. Pray the Lords to call the parties before them.

---

* To be more precise, the lantern, the death mask and the mantle are in the Tradescant Room of the Ashmolean, and the miscellaneous bits of dodo in the Museum of Natural History.

By the end of the century, the problem had grown worse still. To try to combat this, in 1697 the Menagerie issued an advertisement, but a somewhat paranoid, protectionist one that sought to remind potential offenders of the prohibition against rival displays:

> All persons whom it may concern, are desired to take notice,
> That the Master-keeper of his Majesty's Lion-office, in the
> Tower of London, is informed, that several persons do
> expose to publick view several wild beasts, against his
> Majesty's prerogative-royal, and a prohibition given and
> published to the contrary, as in the following, – 'That no
> person whatsoever, (except Thomas Dymocke, and the
> keeper of his Majesty's Lions for the time being) do for the
> future carry abroad, or expose to publick view, for their own
> private gain, any lions, lionesses, leopards, or any other
> beasts which are feroe naturae, as they will answer the
> contrary at their peril.'

Under the pretence of enforcing the law this was not a bad way of doing a little bit of self-promotion; so it went on to mention, as if by-the-by, a few of the items a visitor might hope to see if he were to leave the sordid amusements of the street and come instead to the respectable Tower collection – a hyena, a tiger from the East India Company and so on.

This may have worked as a piece of positive advertising, but as an attempt to prohibit competition it was utterly ineffectual. No amount of heavy-handed warning from the Tower was able to stamp out itinerant or temporary displays, like the West Indies rhinoceros that in 1683 appeared at the Belle Sauvage,* on show for a few days only.

And besides, there was a great deal of perfectly legitimate competition, from a number of collections – condoned by the government and the king – including the eminently respectable 'India House' (as the diplomat and writer Lorenzo Magalotti called it – probably East India House), which was 'full of rare and curious things . . . birds of paradise, a serpent whose size is most remarkable . . . and many other animals and curiosities which came from India and are kept there to gratify the curiosity of the public.'

But with its history, its royal associations (and plenty of royal pocket money spent to maintain it) and the added appeal conferred on it by the excitement and danger of seeing the unpredictable and bloody beasts, alive and close up, for most Londoners it was undoubtedly the Tower that kept the upper hand in this competitive market. Through the eighteenth century it was to remain far and away the most popular tourist attraction in the capital. Its prominence among the other less successful sights of the city had been commemorated some time earlier in the phrase 'going to see the lions,' meaning the highlights, the principal glories of the city. Someone who 'had not even seen the lions,' then, was bound to be from out of town. The phrase was used as early as 1590, in Robert Greene's pamphlet 'Never Too Late': 'Francesco was no other but a meere novice,

---

* The Belle Sauvage, the inn where Pocahontas had stayed, was also the site of the performance of Marlowe's *Dr Faustus* in which rather arrestingly the Devil himself appeared onstage.

and that so newly, that to use the olde proverbe, he had scarce seene the Lions' – and Greene's local readers would have understood (note too that the proverb was by now already considered 'olde'). A decade later, in 1600, a character in Ben Jonson's play *Cynthia's Revels* defends his worldliness, saying valiantly, '[I] will not be frighted with a face, Signior! I have seene the lyons.'

6

Visitors, Novelists, Preachers, Journalists, Fools and Spies

In London City there lived a lady,
Who was possessed of a vast estate,
And she was courted by men of honour,
Lords, dukes and earls on her did wait.

There was two brothers who became lovers,
And both had married this lady fair,
And both to gain her they did endeavour,
And how to please her was all their care.

She ordered her coachman for to get ready,
For to get ready at the break of day;
This lady and her two warlike heroes
To the Tower Hill they did ride away.

And when she came to the Tower Hill,
She threw her fan into the lions' den,
Saying, 'He who wishes to gain my favour
Will bring me back my fan again.'

The Tower Menagerie

Out there spoke the younger brother,
In a voice of thunder both loud and high,
'To hostile danger I am no stranger,
I'll bring you back, love, your fan or die.'

He took his sword and went in among them,
The lions fawned and fell at his feet,
And then he stooped for the fan and got it;
He said, 'Is this it, my darling sweet?'

—Folk song (Anonymous)

Moving on through the second half of the seventeenth century and into the eighteenth, anyone exploring the history of the Tower Menagerie is faced with sudden and significant changes. Not substantive changes to the structure or contents of the Menagerie itself, so much as to the kind and quantity of information to which we have access.

At this point in the story we are, all of a sudden, inundated with unofficial information, information not from the Tower's records or the royal Patent Rolls but from the writings of visitors. Where investigations into the workings of the Menagerie in medieval London have to make broad assumptions and creative leaps based on nothing but the occasional account book or inventory (with the *function* of most writing at this time evident and predictable), we are now overwhelmed with real eyewitness information, synthesized into journals, letters, novels and newspapers. Besides the fact that the number of people visiting the Tower soared, and with it the number of eyewitnesses, there was quite simply an explosion of writing in these decades. Not only did the unique records of Britain's two first and greatest diarists, Samuel Pepys and John Evelyn, provide us with so much of what we know about the detail of their extraordinary worlds; but speedy developments in print technology following Johannes Gutenberg's invention of movable type in the mid–fifteenth century allowed all sorts of new functions of writing to be developed – mass enlightenment and entertainment the most important and striking of these – with the birth of a print culture and the English press.

Since the appearance of the *Weekly News*, Nathaniel Butter's not-actually-weekly digest of continental news, which began in 1621 and was to run irregularly for two decades, it had been possible to disseminate information relatively cheaply and at unprecedented speed to large numbers of people throughout the capital and beyond. And although the first daily paper, the *Daily Courant*, did not appear for another eighty years,* there were sufficient weeklies and occasionals, not to mention all the widely circulated news-pamphlets, newsbooks, newsletters, corantos and news-ballads, to ensure that when it mattered, word could get around (and that there would always be more than enough work for the first generation of English journalists).

The rather less lofty consequence of this great print revolution is that we now have a far more comprehensive record of what was happening at the Tower.

For example, among the earliest recorded visitors to the new and improved People's Tower were Joseph Addison and Richard

---

* Issue 1 appeared on 11 March 1702, three days after the accession of Queen Anne; it was issued by a bookseller based just off Fleet Street, the street that for almost three hundred years was to remain the home ground of the British press.

Steele, the two great political journalists of the early eighteenth century. Together these men founded *Tatler*, an influential (if short-lived) periodical, which after just two years was replaced by the equally influential (and marginally more resilient) *Spectator*[*] and in 1715 by the more overtly political *Freeholder*. Both *Tatler* and *Freeholder* carried stories about the Menagerie, accounts of visits, with first Steele (in *Tatler*) and then Addison (*Freeholder*) describing attempts to enlighten the uninitiated into the joys of watching the royal animals. This is Steele in 1709, describing how he took

> three lads who are under my guardianship a rambling in a hackney-coach to show them the town, as the lions, the tombs, Bedlam and other places which are entertainments to raw minds.

The 'Bedlam' that Steele refers to is the Bethlehem Royal Hospital,[†] the lunatic asylum whose name has since become a generic term for a madhouse. For most of the eighteenth century the hospital was open to members of the public, who were allowed in to be entertained by the behavior of the patients. These unfortunates were kept chained in cells or let out on to galleries to give their paying public a better view. Like the Menagerie, Bedlam drew crowds; and if being gaped at didn't do

---

[*] Neither is directly related to the modern magazine that bears its name.

[†] Since 1675 the hospital had been in a beautiful building at Moorfields (compared by Evelyn to the Tuileries); it was moved in 1815 to new premises in Lambeth, to the building that today houses the Imperial War Museum.

a great deal to speed up patients' recovery, it did at least bring in twopence a head. As Henry III had shown in the building of his multipurpose elephant house, and as the numerous freak shows in the eighteenth century attest, little distinction was drawn between keeping and exhibiting animals and keeping and exhibiting humans who were also worth watching behind bars (as with the sad case of the American Indian kept by James I as part of his collection in St James's Park). Indeed, it would not be long before the Menagerie enclosures would be rebuilt, mirroring a design prototyped for a human prison.

Now here is Addison, in *Freeholder*, around 1715:

> This discourse held us until we came to the Tower; for our first visit was to the lions. My friend, who had a great deal of talk with their keeper, inquired very much after their health, and whether none of them had fallen sick upon the taking of Perth, and the flight of the Pretender? And hearing that they were never better in their lives, I found he was extremely startled; for he had learned from his cradle, that the lions in the Tower were the best judges of the title of our British kings, and always sympathised with our sovereigns.

The friend in Addison's company was his faithful 'Tory fox-hunter,' his regular companion on excursions like these – part sounding board, part straight man. This conservative figure clearly set store by the old superstitions; and this superstition in particular had lately been reinforced by the death of King Charles II and its rumored proximity to that of one of his lions.

This old superstition would take many more years to die. As

late as 1758, when the ageing George II was suffering from a particularly nasty attack of the gout, the politician Lord Chesterfield wrote:

> It was generally thought that H.M. would have died, and for a
> good reason, for the oldest lion in the Tower – much about
> the King's age – died a fortnight ago! This extravagancy, I can
> assure you, was believed by many above the common people.

*

Two changes to society and sensibility led to the explosion of tourism that characterized the next period in the Tower's history.

The first, and for our purposes the less important of the two, was a result of the swift rise in the levels of disposable income in the pockets of average Londoners after the middle of the seventeenth century. This meant that by the eighteenth, London society had become a more consumerist society than ever before.

More important than this was the second change, the rapid growth in ideas of self-improvement; linked to other phenomena such as the birth and expansion of the empire, this trend was fueled by the new press, and led to the setting up of academies across the country, and a sudden rush of people frantic to go and look at things in cabinets and cages that might be educational or otherwise edifying.

The Tower found itself all of a sudden in possession of a marketable commodity. In the wake of the English Civil War and Glorious Revolution (1688–89), new views of national history were forming, and new concepts of national identity had begun to crystallize in the consciousness of enthusiastic and receptive

Britons. This happened nowhere more than in the capital, and all these developments were embodied within that impressive little site on the bank of the Thames. Monarchy, treachery, opulence, rebellion, romance, political activism and dissent, even polar bears. All English life was here. And just waiting to be packaged and sold.

'National Heritage' was not yet valued per se, however; it was certainly not yet enshrined in the rather sterile way it sometimes is today; quite the contrary, people in the eighteenth century were rather casual in their destruction of (for instance) churches that today would be bubble-wrapped in historic-preservation orders and the like. Nonetheless the Tower embodied more than mere heritage, it embodied the nation's very identity, the nation's memory. And the Tower itself recognized this; and through the end of the seventeenth century (with Charles II's crown jewels now on display, of course, besides the animals, the armory, etc.), and as the eighteenth century dawned, it began to sell itself accordingly, with great and rapid success.

The Tower was no longer properly a royal palace (so visitors in large numbers did not pose the security risk they would have a couple of centuries earlier, in the reign of Henry VIII, for instance); and only rarely was it now used as a prison (the days following the Gordon Riots in 1780 being one of very few exceptions); so its role as a repository of the trappings of monarchy (animals included), as a repository of historical artifacts and of history itself, could be emphasized.

The Tower didn't go so far as to produce its own guidebooks yet, though even this was not long distant (the first, illustrated and designed for children, appeared in 1741), but at least the Tower

AN

HISTORICAL DESCRIPTION

Thomas OF THE *Baker*

TOWER of LONDON,

AND ITS

CURIOSITIES.

Giving an ACCOUNT

1. Of its Foundation, gradual Encreafe, and prefent State.
2. Of its Government, Cuftoms, and Privileges.
3. Of its Antiquities, Records, and Curiofities.
4. Of the Lions, and other wild Beafts kept there; their Nature and Properties.
5. Of the Spoils of the *Spanifh* Armada, with the Hiftory of the *Spanifh* Invafion in 1588.
6. Of the Small Armory; in which, at one View, may be feen Arms for 80,000 Men.

7. Of the Royal Train of Artillery; comprehending the various Engines of Deftruction ufed in War.
8. Of the Horfe-Armory; with curious Anecdotes relating to the Kings that fit there on Horfeback in full Armour, from *William the Conqueror*, to the late King *George*.
9. Of the Jewel-Office, and the Regalia, ufed at the Coronation of our Kings; and the Story of Col. *Blood*'s attempting to fteal away the Crown.
10. Of the Mint, and the Manner of ftamping Money.

Written chiefly to direct the Attention of Spectators to what is moft curious in this Repofitory, and to enable them afterwards to relate what they have feen.

LONDON:

Printed for J. NEWBERY, at the *Bible* and *Sun* in St. *Paul's Church-Yard.* Price Six pence.

M DCC LXVII.

and its animals featured prominently in general guides to London, both English and foreign. One early guide, Allain Manesson Mallet's ambitiously titled *Description de l'univers*, published in France in 1683, has this description of the animals under the last Stuart, James II:

> In the part of the Castle overlooking the river is a place set
> aside for the keeping of wild beasts of all kinds. Close to this
> is a sort of chasm, or abyss filled with water. This is where
> they throw those who have betrayed the country. It was here
> that they threw a part of the corpse of Cromwell.

The most complete record of the visitor experience of the Menagerie in this period comes directly from a visitor's mouth, from the tavern-keeper and occasional (but sometimes tiresomely prolific) writer Ned Ward, in the *London Spy*. Ward's grumpy narrator, the Spy, describes a visit he and a companion made to the Tower in the winter of 1699.

They first passed a sign indicating that they were approaching the collection of wild beasts; the sign showed a lion's head, though the Spy thought 'it seemed the picture of some rugged-faced man's head' and 'compared it in my thoughts to everybody I could recollect' without quite being able to identify it.

Undaunted, he and his companion were led into the lion yard:

> . . . we went in, where the yard smelt as frowzily as a dove-
> house or a dog-kennel. In their separate apartments were
> four of their stern affrighting catships, one with a whelp

presented to His late Majesty, of which the dam was as fond
as an old maid, when married, is of her first child; one
couchant, another dormant, a third passant gardant, a
fourth, very fierce, was rampant, being a lioness. . . . She put
out her paw to me, which was tipped with such ill-favoured
sort of pruning-hooks, that rather than she should have
shaken me by the hand I would have chosen to have taken
Old Nick by his cloven foot, and should have thought myself
in less danger.

The Spy also notices two other lions, but is dismayed to find
them

dead and their skins stuffed, one of them having been King
Charles's lion, but had no more fierceness in his looks that he
had when he was living, than the effigy of his good master at
Westminster has the presence of the original. The other that
was stuffed was said to be Queen Mary's, but made such a
drooping figure with his false entrails, that it brought into my
mind an old proverb . . . that a living dog is better than a
dead lion.

The next ill-favoured creatures that were presented to our
sight were a couple of pretty looking hell-cats, called a tiger,
and a catamountain, whose fierce penetrating eyes pierced
through my belly to the sad gripping of my guts, as if,
basilisk-like, they could have killed at a distance with their
very looks.

In another apartment or ward, for the convenience of

drawing a penny more out of the pocket of a spectator, [is placed] a leopard, who is grown as cunning as a cross Bedlamite that loves not to be looked at. For as the madman will be apt to salute you with a bowl of chamber-lie, so will the leopard, if you come near him, stare in your face and piss upon you, his urine being as hot as aqua fortis, and stinks worse than a polecat's.

They are shown three eagles, two owls ('outlandish') and a hyena, none of which succeeds in impressing the Spy any more than the wildcats have. In fact, of his whole visit to the Tower, the only thing that impresses him is John of Gaunt's codpiece, 'which was almost as big as a poop-lantern, and better worth a lewd lady's admiration than any piece of antiquity in the Tower.'

Another visitor of around this time, the Swiss traveler César de Saussure (writing in 1725), was no more impressed than Ward at the enclosures the animals were being kept in ('small and rather dirty'); but unlike the Spy he did particularly enjoy one animal attraction: 'What amused us most was the sight of four young lions a few months old, born in the Tower, and they were too young to be ferocious, they allowed us to fondle and caress them as if they had been little dogs.'

Although public access was beginning to become the *raison d'être* for the Tower animals, visits were never entirely without hazard, and the more careless could find themselves seriously at risk. Most unfortunate is the fate of the young and foolhardy Norfolk girl Mary Jenkinson. In 1686 the heroine of this cautionary tale (a girl 'extracted of honest parents' moreover) had for a time been 'living with the Person who keeps the Lyons,' and so was a frequent visitor to their cages. But on one terrible occasion,

> going into the Den to show them to some Acquaintance of hers, one [of] the Lyons (being the greatest there), putting out his Paw, she was so venturous as to stroke him as she used to do, but suddenly he catched her by the middle of the Arm with his Claws and mouth, and most miserably tore her Flesh from the Bone, before he could be unloosed, notwithstanding they thrust several lighted Torches at him, but at last they got her away, whereupon chirurgeons were immediately called for, who after some time thought it necessary for the preservation of her Life, to cut off her Arm, but she Died not many Hours after, to the great Grief of her Friends here in Town; which Example ought to remind every good Christian to consider their latter End before they go hence, and be no more seen.

These were strange, barely understood creatures the keepers were dealing with, and no amount of prior experience of their habits and behavior (after all, by this time wildcats had been arriving quite regularly at the Tower for almost five hundred years) seemed to make them any more predictable than King John's had been. But we can at least console ourselves that since this incident was considered worthy of report in the contemporary pamphlet whence derives that rather touching – and rather sprawling –

sentence quoted, at least such things can not have been commonplace.

Such incidents did nothing to deter many out-of-town visitors from making for the lions at the first opportunity. It was known up and down the country that when – if – one made it to the capital, on a visit to a metropolitan cousin perhaps, or to collect merchandise to trade, the Tower must be the first port of call.

In his novel *The History of Henry Esmond*, set in the reign of Queen Anne, Thackeray sends his young hero Henry down to London, where his conscientious tutor makes sure he introduces him to all the (not excessively corrupting) delights the capital has to offer:

> He will remember to his life's end the delights of those days.
> He was taken to see a play by Monsieur Blaise, in a house a
> thousand times greater and finer than the booth at Ealing
> Fair – and on the next happy day they took water at the
> river, and Harry saw London Bridge with the houses and
> booksellers' shops thereon, looking like a street, and the
> Tower of London, with the armour, and the great lions and
> bears in the moats . . .

Henry Esmond was written long after the closure of the Menagerie, of course, but it was – indeed still is – common for historical novelists to use references to it as a kind of historical shorthand, providing instant period color. Historical fiction that was written after the dismantling of the Menagerie but refers to it in this way ranges from Ainsworth's mid-nineteenth-century novel *Tower of*

London through T. H. White's classic Arthurian fantasy *The Once and Future King*, to any number of novels of the very recent past.[*]

The Tower animals were still considered a vital part of every conscientious tourist's itinerary as late as 1760, when Smollett was writing *Humphry Clinker*. The maidservant Winifred Jenkins reports:

> Last week I went with my mistress to the Tower, to see the crowns and wild beastis; and there was a monstracious lion, with teeth half a quarter [nine inches] long; and a gentleman bid me not go near him, if I wasn't a maid, being as how he would roar, and tear, and play the dickens – Now I had no mind to go near him; for I cannot abide such dangerous honeymils, not I – but my mistress would go; and the beast kept such a roaring and bouncing, that I tho't he would have broke his cage and devoured us all; and the gentleman tittered forsooth; but I'll go to death upon it, I will, that my lady is as good a firchin, as the child unborn; and therefore, either the old gentleman told a fib, or the lion oft to be set in the stock for bearing false witness against his neighbour; for the commandment sayeth, thou shalt not bear false witness against thy neighbour.

---

[*] I have come across half a dozen such books published in the last few years alone, spanning all kinds of fiction, for adults and children alike. For the record they are *The House of Sight and Shadow* (Nicholas Griffin, 2000); *According to Queeney* (Beryl Bainbridge, 2001); *Widow's Kiss* (Jane Feather, 2001), *A Handful of Magic* (Stephen Elboz, 2000), *The Shakespeare Stealer* (Gary Blackwood, 1999); *The Giant O'Brien* (Hilary Mantel, 1998).

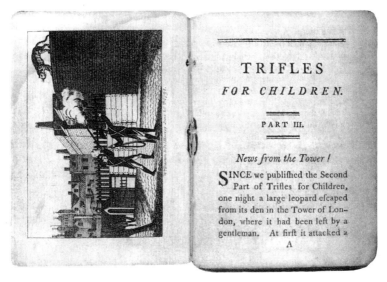

TRIFLES

FOR CHILDREN.

PART III.

News from the Tower !

SINCE we publiſhed the Second Part of Trifles for Children, one night a large leopard eſcaped from its den in the Tower of London, where it had been left by a gentleman. At firſt it attacked a

A

Illustration from an eighteenth-century children's book, describing the escape of one of the Tower leopards.

Smollett's novel and the journalists' articles help to mark the almost imperceptible drift of the Menagerie into London's cultural language, with more and more traditions and superstitions springing up around it. Besides the theory that the Tower lions could identify whether or not a woman was a virgin (which was, as in *Humphry Clinker*, a potentially very embarrassing talent) and the old (but still not discredited) tradition of lions' and monarchs' lives being profoundly linked, there was also the belief that the Tower lions were particularly attuned to the weather on Candlemas Day, as if they too knew that proverbially:

The Tower Menagerie

If Candlemas Day be fair and bright
Winter will have another flight.

So when the second of February came around and the weather was glorious, the prospect of a longer winter would be expected to drive the lions into a state of profound depression. In the final scene of John Webster's *The White Devil*, his character Flamineo refers to 'the lions i' th' Tower on Candlemas day, [that] mourn if the sun shine for fear of the pitiful remainder of winter to come.'

The spring of 1698 saw the appearance of a new tradition, and one that was to be particularly persistent. A rumor began to circulate that the Tower lions were to be washed in the moat on April the first, and that tickets were to be sold for this event. A few people even received personal invitations, gilt-edged. And of course many turned up to see the spectacle, only to be told that, yes, it was April Fools' Day and that the keepers had no intention of doing anything so foolish. From that year on, the Washing of the Lions was advertised for April the first on a regular basis, and every time troops of the unsuspecting – mainly tourists, for Londoners learned the truth fast – turned up at the Tower only to be told that they had fallen for what eventually became an old, old joke. This practice was taken yet further in some years, when someone went so far as to print tickets for the washing ceremony.

In 1771, when this had been going on for three quarters of a century, the following account appeared:

Yesterday being April day, two men went to the Tower to see the annual ceremony of washing the lions; on enquiry what time they would be washed, they were told, by a waterman, in about ten minutes; he at the same time advised them to have a boat, as they might see better on the water: they had no sooner got into the boat but the waterman pushed them off, without any oars, and being immediately surrounded by a number of watermen in their boats, were well splashed by them for almost a quarter of an hour, to the great diversion of the spectators.

Having infiltrated London's cultural awareness, the Tower Menagerie quickly became a useful tool for satirists and caricaturists; as with all cultural references, they used it as a kind of shorthand for all sorts of things.

For example, when in 1714 Queen Anne died, a poem appeared – as if from nowhere – that made it quite clear that her successor, the distinctly foreign George I, was not a welcome arrival in the country. For obvious reasons (its target was the acceding king, after all) this piece of satire was anonymous, claiming to have been written by the Tower of London itself.

The arrival of a new king – especially the one even now on his way over from Germany – was likely to bring trouble. The people's alarm and that of the Church were not shared by the Tower, however, says the poem, as for six centuries Trouble had been precisely the Tower's *raison d'être*. In fact the place sounds positively gleeful:

To the K——g's Most Excellent M———y,
The Humble Address of the TOWER OF LONDON

Dread SIR,

Let *England*'s Church her sinking State deplore,
And vainly weep, now ANNA is no more:
Too late grown Wise, let *Tories* think, with Tears,
How ill they Husbanded Four fruitful Years;
Let *Britain* too lament, her Freedom lost
And think how Dear a *German* K——g hath cost.
Just is my joy! My Transports are sincere!
Thee *G*——*e*, I welcome! Thee my Walls revere!
Thy *Gothick*, *Turkish* Rule, proclaims my Power,
In ancient Tower, reinstates the *Tower*.

No more shall gaping *Cits*, and staring *Clowns*
With awkward Jests, deride my harmless Guns:
No longer shall my idle Axes rust,
Or massive Chains lie Useless in the Dust:
No more shall tender Dam'sels flock to see
My Lyons, far less Terrible than Thee!
Their Dens shall now be stock'd with Human Prey!
And bones of Slaughter'd Nobles Pave the Way.

It was probably just as well for the authors of this poem, whoever they were, that the new king spoke no English.

As it happened, the start of the new reign and the appearance on the scene of the Hanovers did indeed herald the beginning of a fruitful period for the Menagerie. The whole visitor experience became steadily more formalized, with set admission prices, which most gratifyingly rose from 3*d* (or, of course, a dog or a cat), to 6*d* (bringing it level with the admission to the Ark), to 9*d*, to a shilling, over the century, and the publication of popular and regularly updated guidebooks.

One of these visitors was the winter-cloaked old John Wesley, flowing white locks and flute-player and all, in to test the king's animals for any sign of a divine soul. And Wesley was by no means the only preacher making a case for compassion towards animals. Among the others taking up the cause was Humphry Primatt, a Norfolk vicar who in 1776 published *The Duty of Mercy and the Sin of Cruelty to Brute Animals*; his argument in this work is based not on science or ethics but precisely on religion – if God is merciful to us, then should we not by example be merciful to animals? After all, 'an animal [is] no less sensible of pain than a man.' The argument is similar to that made by Coleridge's Ancient Mariner in his odd little motto at the closing of the poem:

> Farewell, farewell! but this I tell
> To thee, thou Wedding-Guest!
> He prayeth well, who loveth well
> Both man and bird and beast.
>
> He prayeth best, who loveth best
> All things both great and small;
> For the dear God who loveth us,
> He made and loveth all.

As the years went by, so many preachers took up Primatt's compassionate refrain that when the first animal cruelty bill finally came before Parliament in 1822, the MP who sponsored it, Richard Martin, could claim: 'There was not a pulpit in London that had not spoken in favour of it.' For one thing, animals were given responsibility for their own actions (animal trials had long been common on the continent); and with responsibilities, rights should surely follow.

Killing for food or clothing remained quite another matter, however, and quite acceptable. The poet William Cowper, writing in the decade before Coleridge penned his *Ancient Mariner*, summed up the guidelines thus:

> The sum is this: if man's convenience, health,
> Or safety interfere, his rights and claims
> Are paramount, and must extinguish theirs.
> Else they are all – the meanest things that are –
> As free to live, and to enjoy that life,
> As God was free to form them at the first,
> Who in his sovereign wisdom made them all.*

---

* This subject raises an enormous issue that I do not want to go into here, but is worth making mention of: not only was nobody sure quite how highly to rate the spiritual status of animals, the same question was asked about humans with varying answers depending on whether the humans were male or female, whether they were children, or whether they were slaves. Blake wrote that 'Every thing that lives is Holy,' but the idea that slaves should be so sophisticated and worthwhile as to have a soul would still have been a matter for some dispute at this time.

Not many years after his visit to the Tower, one of Wesley's Menagerie lions died. We do not know, alas, whether it was this animal that had shown such promise in attending so politely to Wesley's flute, nor can we know with any certainty whether the immortal soul of this animal survived, and if so where precisely; Wesley's attempt to answer this question remained incomplete, to say the least. What we do know for sure is that the mortal remains of this animal contributed in some small way to the development of modern surgery and anatomical science. His carcass, still warm, was packed up and transported over to Earls Court, where John Hunter, the Scottish father of surgery, took it apart in the interests of science and the Enlightenment.

7
Science and Sensibility

You ask me why the Brutes should be
As liable to pain as we,
Since they have not a heavenly rest
Nor suffer here to rise more blessed . . .

—Lady Annabella Byron

Walking southwest across the gardens at Lincoln's Inn Fields – the heart of the old English judiciary – you will find yourself approaching a bulky new likeness of the great man of science, the Scottish surgeon and anatomist John Hunter. Walking out of the southern gate of the gardens brings you up to the façade of the Royal College of Surgeons of London, an unremarkable building with a reasonably attractive neoclassical portico, but otherwise hardly worth noticing so close to so many striking Gothic chambers and cloisters and towers, remnants of Palladian houses, a medieval gatehouse, grand Georgian terraces and more.

Once inside the marble-floored entrance hall (notice the large statue of Hunter, again, seated straight ahead of you), you turn left up a grand staircase from over which past presidents of the College look down at passersby – the portraits of the twentieth-century incumbents largely smiling, quite benignly, the busts of their predecessors far more austere, each with a peevish expression suggesting that the sculptor had interrupted him (for they are, of course, all men) at a crucial moment in his work, earthshaking work, needless to say, which is now jeopardized. This brings you to the first floor, part of which houses one of the more extraordinary of London's many and varied private collections, the Hunterian Museum.

In his will John Hunter had specified that his collection was to be offered for sale to the government, for the benefit of the nation; but Pitt, the young prime minister, was doubtful that it was a sufficiently worthwhile acquisition with which to burden the persistently overstretched public purse (there was a war on with France, after all), and refused to authorize the purchase. This is not unforgivable, for few at the time recognized the significance of the collection; even Hunter's friend the great botanist Joseph Banks wrote in January 1796:

> Had I thought my friend John Hunter's collection an object of importance to the general study of natural history, or indeed to any kind of science except to that of medicine, I hope that two years would not have elapsed without my taking an active part in recommending to the public the measure of purchasing it.

It was only some years later, in 1799, that a standing committee decided that government funds should be allocated for this worthy purchase after all, and the collection passed into the keeping of the Company of Surgeons (now the Royal College of Surgeons). For their £15,000 (today some $1.5 million) the Company of Surgeons acquired the most extensive and significant collection of physiological specimens in the country, with 13,682 preparations, in endless jars and bottles in endless cabinets. Some thirty-five hundred specimens from this original collection have survived – including pieces of the animals from the King's Menagerie in the Tower.

The entrance to the museum, at the top of the RCS staircase, is flanked by two portraits: on the right, a Robert Home portrait of John Hunter, painted in the mid-1770s, shortly after Hunter's marriage to Home's sister Anne (an acquaintance of the composer Joseph Haydn, who set some of her writing to music); on the right, Joshua Reynolds's portrait (a copy, in fact) of John's elder, and perhaps underappreciated, brother William. It was William who was the first to leave the family home in Long Calderwood, outside Glasgow, to come down to London to become a surgeon's pupil at the old St George's Hospital on Hyde Park Corner. The year was 1741. By the time his younger brother John joined him in the capital seven years later, William was already established as a prominent physician, surgeon and midwife.

These were the days when the kind of professional medicine we would recognize today was still very much in its infancy. Bleeding was still the most commonly prescribed treatment, and surgery, such as it was, was carried out by near-amateurs without the benefit (to themselves or their patients) of any anesthetic[*] –

---

[*] The first anesthetic was not administered in England until 1846.

the (relatively) luckier patients were given a swig of something strongly alcoholic to take the edge off the pain when, say, having a limb removed, and just had to hope that they might pass out. In 1540 Henry VIII had amalgamated the Company of Surgeons with the Company of Barbers; and for centuries no one but barbers – based at their Hall in Monkwell Street in the City[*] – were allowed to practice surgery.[†] This was still the case when William Hunter began his apprenticeship in London in the early 1740s.

Young John Hunter believed strongly in the value of experiment not just for its own sake but as a teaching tool too. But it was not an easy matter to get human specimens for experimentation; few of the living were prepared to subject themselves to too close scrutiny (remember, still no anesthetics), and graverobbing, while commonplace, was still illegal.[‡] Since 1752 the bodies of executed criminals had been passed on to waiting sur-

---

[*] The street where half a century later a young Shakespeare was to make his home; also yards from the site where John Wesley had the revelation that led to his founding of the Methodist church.

[†] The tradition of surgery being performed not by doctors but by those without university training has its echoes in practice today; even now, when surgeons have to complete their basic medical training before embarking on their specialty, they are still addressed as 'Mister' (or Mrs, Ms) and not 'Doctor.' Tradition has it that the red and white bands on barbershop poles also echo this historically joint role, white for shaving foam and red for blood.

[‡] Though one of Hunter's most famous bodies came to him in a manner even less edifying than common grave-robbing. The very, very tall Charles Byrne, known as the 'Irish Giant,' was during his own lifetime regularly exhibited in the London fairs; Hunter decided he would like the opportunity to investigate this phenomenon, and offered the Giant a lump sum to sign over the rights to his body *post mortem*. Byrne declined. After Byrne's death Hunter contacted the man

geons for their experiments, but with the proliferation of the experimentally inclined there were simply not enough bodies to go around. The situation changed with the 1832 Anatomy Act, which made workhouse bodies available for dissection, but this came far too late for John Hunter. So upon arrival in London he decided to supplement his meager quota of legal human cadavers (a perk of working at St George's) with animals; from these animal specimens, dissected and examined, he hoped to be able by extension to draw conclusions about human anatomy and physiology. Hunter learnt a lot from the great comparative anatomists who had gone before him, from Aristotle onwards; and although it was not appreciated at the time, he and his collection made a significant contribution to the development of this ancient science. It is worth noting, though, that many of Galen's mistakes had arisen because he had studied animals, Barbary apes and the like, and drawn incorrect assumptions about humans from them, such as his oft-quoted reference to the *rete mirabile* (a cluster of veins at the back of the neck at the base of the brain stem), which is to be found in sheep but not in humans; what then had made the Flemish physician and anatomist Vesalius remarkable, a full fourteen centuries later, was the fact that he had actually looked at people themselves. But for the most part animals would have to do for Hunter.

---

who was to dispose of the body according to the dead man's wishes, and an arrangement was reached; the upshot of which is that the skeleton of the Irish Giant is still on view at the Hunterian today. Byrne was certainly a special case, though, and for an average body such elaborate dealings just wouldn't have been worth Hunter's money or such trouble.

Soon an arrangement was made with the keeper of the king's animals, John Ellys, whereby first refusal of all cadavers from the Tower Menagerie should be given to Mr Hunter. It remains unclear whether this arrangement was entirely above board or whether, as seems more probable, it was a back-door supplement to Ellys's income. It isn't hard to imagine the body of some unfortunate, recently deceased gazelle, hyena or the like being wedged into a burlap bag and taken down to Kew (in those days a village outside London) in the dead of night, then left hastily on Mr Hunter's doorstep with a scribbled note and invoice pinned to it.

Hunter made the most of the bodies Ellys supplied him with; not a piece was wasted. Through the 1750s he did exhaustive studies on animals' dentition, respiratory systems, reproductive organs and circulation. Elephants, tigers, lions, rhinos and more were all hauled, still warm, out of the Menagerie and onto his dissection table; they provided him with a focus for his observations and experiments, and in return he immortalized them, in formaldehyde. Most of the larger animal skeletons from this collection were destroyed in the bomb damage of World War II, but several thousand other specimens survive on view at Lincoln's Inn Fields today.

Hunter kept houses in Leicester Square and at Earls Court. He used the former for teaching, so did some dissecting work there; but it was in Earls Court that he had his own menagerie, and where all the larger dissections were done, so it's likely that the Tower animals were brought here for his investigations. In all he dissected over five hundred species.

Hunter's experimental investigation on animals was based on the precept that form follows function, that by examining an anatomical feature it would be possible to make significant deductions about its workings. As was shown with Galen, making deductions about humans based on experiments on animals is far from ideal, but in Hunter's case there were numerous ways in which such experiments were able to make important contributions to his work on the specifics of anatomy and to his development of surgery in general.

Hunter's own menagerie was quite extensive for a private collection, which is unsurprising given his dedication to keeping it well stocked. Every time he scraped together a few coins, it was said, he would rush off and buy some new specimen with them. When he didn't have the money himself he would simply find a friend to borrow from. Besides the animals themselves (which were a good investment, in that he knew he would find a use for them dead as well as alive), he assembled an impressive collection of pictures of animals too. He may have been a reasonably good artist himself, but among those he employed to do pictures to commission were some of the very best in the business. Even George Stubbs produced a painting of a newly arrived rhinoceros for him, a painting still on display in the museum today (see plate 7). The usefulness to Hunter of his own scientific drawings and those he commissioned was dependent not on their aesthetic value, but on their cold, pragmatic accuracy. These pictures would not delight the eye, perhaps, but they would help him in his studies, help him to understand how things worked, help him to make sense of it all. The master-draughtsman Stubbs was most unusual in his ability to create a work both scientifically accurate and aesthetically pleasing.

The rise of investigative science as something not just independently interesting but actually useful and desirable was linked – symbolically – to another great movement exactly contemporary with it. Understanding brings greater power, as is well known, it brings greater control, and never before had the idea that Nature would be best if she could only be properly controlled been so fashionable. Nature was there to be ordered, to be tamed. Animals should be caged for observation, animal species identified and labeled; plants likewise identified and categorized and put symbolically in their place. Gardens should not be left to run wild but they too should be tamed, brought into order – hence the appearance in these decades of the great landscape gardeners, first Brown and then Repton, who took messy Nature in hand and made her do what they wanted her to do. It was now too, while Hunter was trying to resolve some of the complexities of animal physiology, that the roaming deer park at Woodstock became the precious piece of manicuring we see at Blenheim today.

There was still a strong public sense of not-quite-normal-ness about the animals, a sense of unease, and certainly a great deal of fear associated with interacting with them too – and besides this the suspicion that our so-called control over Nature is only ever a hairsbreadth away from total anarchy, that every beast contained in a cage is a wild-beast-running-rampant just waiting to happen. So it is hardly surprising that as the Gordon Riots began to sweep across the capital in June 1780 (Lincoln's Inn Fields, home now to Hunter's collection, being one of the most serious flashpoints) a rumor began to circulate that the rioters planned to release the wild beasts from the Tower and the lunatics from the Bedlam just to add to the general chaos. Fear of the monstrous creatures in the Tower, and a similar terror of the equally incomprehensible inmates of the mental hospital, was being used as a weapon, just as it had helped to deter potential invaders of the Tower centuries earlier. And added to the very real fear that the rioters were playing on was the potent symbolic value of this threatened gesture: in one move, a breaching of the king's great fortress (like the Peasants' Revolt), an overruling of royal authority and justice (the storming of the Bastille), a looting of the king's own much-loved personal possessions (as symbolic as Blood's attempt on the Crown Jewels). According to Walpole this latest threat was no less than 'diabolical.'

The fear was born of an inability to understand and identify, and as long as this was the case there was room for extensive experiment and enquiry, by Hunter and others. There was even enquiry of sorts in the Tower itself. Some suffered from this phase of manic experimentation. Animals had no rights, no say in how they were to be experimented on – many died horribly painful deaths as a result. It had long been believed, for instance, that ostriches were able to digest iron (a belief originating in a French bestiary; the Queen Mary Psalter shows an ostrich being fed horseshoes); in the early 1590s Shakespeare had given one of his characters (Jack Cade in *Henry VI, Part II*) the threat 'I'll make thee eat iron like an ostrich, and swallow my sword like a great pin, ere thou and I part.' The Tower guidebooks published in the 1750s stated rather smugly that some people in Holland (in 1659) had been foolish enough to believe an ostrich capable of this feat ('a vulgar error'), so of course their ostrich died, and when opened, its stomach was found to contain dozens of nails, all 'intact' (i.e., undigested). Besides refuting this common misconception, Maitland wrote in

1751 that this proves the birds' 'Voraciousness and Stupidity, which makes this animal swallow Things prejudicial to its Life.' And yet the rumor did linger;[*] and when in 1791 George III and the Tower received yet another ostrich, the Tower staff saw it as a perfect opportunity to put this theory to the test. Unsurprisingly the ostrich died fairly promptly; upon dissection it was found to have swallowed more than eighty nails.

There is a crucial difference between a misconception such as this and those we saw a few centuries earlier, like the sad case of the elephant that was given only wine to drink. In the case of the elephant, the keepers were given their instructions, they followed them, the elephant died and nobody knew why (any number of things could have killed it, they thought) – and as a result nothing was learnt from the experience. With the ostrich the feeding of the nails was done precisely as an experiment, in order to learn the answer to a long-disputed issue, and the result was unambiguous and the lesson (one hopes) learned.

This new mood of enquiry clearly did not do this particular ostrich any good, but in many cases led to answers that had useful practical application for the Menagerie. It was now, for instance, that it was possible for the first time to breed animals successfully within it. Though lions had been bred under James I, none had survived any length of time (besides, any that survived infancy would only have been made fodder for James's bloody sporting

---

[*] For all the guidebook's smugness, one of the two ostriches donated by the dey of Tunis had died in the Tower, just a few months earlier, having swallowed a large nail that 'stopt its passage.'

tastes). By the 1750s, knowledge about how to keep the animals had advanced to the extent that cubs were now surviving into adulthood; and it was claimed in the guidebooks that 'so much knowledge has been acquired of the art of rearing them, that we may boast now of an uninterrupted line of British lions.'

This is interesting particularly in the light of those comments back in James I's reign to the effect that the only animal nobler than a lion is a British animal. And now we have British lions – what could be greater?

Besides the fact that knowledge was being newly gathered, there was the fact that this knowledge was also being efficiently disseminated for the first time, and before long guidebooks to the Tower began to include more and more (and more accurate) information about the animals visitors were seeing. The mere fact that information of this kind was provided at all is striking – visitors no longer want simply to be impressed, excited, astonished, but to learn too, to be educated and improved.

The very first such guidebook, a two-volume affair called *Curiosities in the Tower of London*, published in 1741 (priced at 4*d*), was aimed – remarkably – at a readership of children, and was not only educational but entertaining too. As befitted books for young readers (the list of 'Subscribers' at the beginning is made up entirely of Masters and Misses), at under 6 centimeters – some 2⅜ inches – tall they are about the smallest books you could ever hope to see.

The book includes not only descriptions of the animals, usually by name, but also charming (if unsophisticated) pictures of each of the species (caged) to be found in the collection. It begins with a bit of reassurance for those of a nervous disposition:

LION.

The wild creatures that are there shewn are all kept in strong dens, so that you need not be under any fear of danger from them; – Don't venture too near, and you may view them very safely. The dens are made in the form in which the pictures represent; in which are two rooms; the lower has strong thick bars of wood, the upper, iron: in one of which the keeper secures the creature, whilst the other is clean'd, &c.

So what could a child reading this book in 1741 expect to see on a visit to the Menagerie?

First of all, the two lionesses, Jenny and Phillis, and the lion Marco ('consort to Phillis'); a leopard called Will and a panther called Jenny; two tigers (Will and Phillis); then a racoon, two vultures and two eagles, for whom we are not given a name (though if the names of the big cats are any clue, we might not be missing much).

In another area (for which a further admission fee is required) is the lioness Nanny, and many of the smaller creatures: among them a porcupine, an ape, three lion cubs called Priscilla, Pompey (whom we shall meet again) and Nell; the tiger cub Dick (son of

The APE.

Will II and Phillis II), and the lion cub 'young prince Nero'* (son to Marco and Phillis I).

---

* 'My young readers will excuse my not giving them the picture of prince Nero, because he is so like his papa, whose royal visage you may see in page 34, that it would appear almost the same.'

There was also 'an uncommon, large, beautiful Bird, called Warwoven, or King of the Vawous. It was brought to the Tower in September last, and was a present from his grace the Duke of Mountagu. It is somewhat lesser than the Eagle. These kinds of birds are found in some parts of the East-Indies.'

PORCUPINE.

> Lions, Tigers, Panthers and Leopards, are fed sheeps heads and plucks* twice a day; of which a Lion eats four or five in a day; but Leopards, Panthers, and Tigers, are much fonder of raw dogs-flesh. They drink as often as they please. Usually several times in a day; each having a stone trough in his den.

It was, at last, a good time for the Menagerie. Conditions had been poor for much of the first half of the century, with most of the Menagerie accommodations severely overcrowded; the result was a high mortality rate, and a rapid turnover of animals. But by the 1770s and 1780s, as conditions began to be improved, the number of animals was rising again. People were prepared to go to great lengths to get them too; in 1775, for instance, the acqui-sition of a lion in Senegal cost two human lives. A perturbed *Gentleman's Magazine* reported that the lion 'was

THIS PAGE AND OPPOSITE
Woodcuts from the 1741 children's guide to the Tower, Curiosities in the Tower of London.

EAGLE.

---

* Heart, lungs, liver, etc., a word usually used with reference to these organs' use as food.

taken in the woods out of a snare, by a private soldier, who being set upon by two savages that had laid the snare, he killed both, and brought away his game.'

The magazine points out that 'killing two innocent fellow-creatures, *unprovoked*, only to rob them of the fruits of their ingenuity, can never surely be accounted *meritorious* in one who calls himself a Christian'; and one correspondent asks: 'In the name of all that is sacred, is a lion's whelp an equivalent with the K. of England for the lives of two human creatures?' Apparently so, according to the king, who 'for [the soldier's] bravery, has ordered his discharge, and a pension for life of 5ol a year.'

When this young lion cub reached London he would have been pleased to find conditions in the Tower improving markedly. To begin with the dens were being fully refurbished (as was the keeper's house); a few years later further building work was to take place, improving the old cages (replacing the wooden floors with brick, installing a system of flues to keep the cages relatively warm in winter) and constructing new ones.

But – new heating system or not – the animals still could not be said to be happy. The cages, even extensively modernized, still measured about 10 feet across, barely enough room for a big cat to turn around in. Descriptions of their 'natures' as perceived by those who had only ever seen them captive may give us a clue to how comfortable the animals were in their homes, and how satisfactory the conditions were; it was said, for example, that 'the lion in the daytime, seems to be a very sluggish, heavy animal, that hates to be rous'd, and is no sooner up, but, if suffer'd, will immediately flap down again.' It is true that even lions in the wild spend what seems like a self-indulgent proportion of their days asleep, but the description of a waking lion as a rather lazy, dull thing is telling. But sad as this description is, it is only what one would expect; this place was not made to optimize the experience of the animals, it was made for visitors, and the visitor experience was planned through in an exemplary fashion. It is described in full in a visitors' guide to the Tower published in 1755:

> Over the door where you are to enter is the figure of a lion; there you ring, and for Sixpence each Person, you will presently gain Admittance, and be shown such a noble Collection of wild Creatures as is well worth any Person's While to spend a few Minutes in admiring.

And so the tour begins:

> At your entrance, you are carried into a Range of Dens in the Form of a Half Moon, some of them empty, and some of them inhabited by Lionesses of different Ages and Accomplishments.
>
> But before your Guides enter upon descriptions of these noble beasts, they take you to the Corner of the Range upon the Left, and shew you what they call the School of Apes, which consists of two Egyptian Nightwalkers and two Apes from Turky. Of the largest of these Creatures they tell you abundance of very surprising Stories; and indeed these sort of Animals are capable of such Variety of droll Imitations of human Actions, that their whimsical Tricks, were they to be remembered, would fill a volume.

Next, you are shown the eight-year-old lioness Dido ('the keeper assured me she was still a Virgin, and therefore her story cannot afford much Entertainment'), another called Jenny (aged just four), and a third called Helen (seven, 'a Virgin indeed, but ready to be matched to the first Suitor'). Thence to the tigers and leopards, then 'a Variety of Royal and other rare Birds, as well as Beasts,' among them 'a Golden Eagle, a noble Bird that has been an Inhabitant here above 90 Years,' apparently, and a horned Owl ('rare and wonderful'!), the great lion Pompey (now fifteen, whom we last saw with sisters Priscilla and Nell when they were just a few months old), a young 'Man Tyger,' one of the ostriches from the dey of Tunis (the one whose 'stupidity' at eating iron nails didn't kill him), a couple of hyenas, a raccoon . . .

Perhaps the most delinquent of these animals at this time was the baboon: 'He has an admirable Art of throwing Stones, and will throw any Lead or Iron that happens to be within his Reach, with such Force as to split Stools, Bowls or any such wooden Utensils in a hundred Pieces.' His guests must have loved that. He was infantile, but funny and endearing too. He was also notorious, for on his journey across to England he had killed a young boy aboard the ship by 'throwing a Cannon Shot of nine Pounds Weight at him, upon some Disgust' – which made him even more interesting, and probably a real crowd-puller, if rather less endearing than he used to be considered.* Nor is it worth trying to beat him at his own game, for we are told that 'if you fling any thing at him you cannot hurt him; for he catches whatever you throw there, with great Dexterity.'

---

* Likewise another of his quirks of behavior: 'He is very young, but by his Motions when Women approach him, appears to be leacherous to a surprising Degree.'

A visitor could see all this, as well as the Armoury and the Crown Jewels, for an entrance fee of 6*d* (about $4.60 today). By 1771 a higher rate of admission had been established, reflecting the more exciting and better presented sights being paid for. And the public were more than happy to pay the higher price.

These new rates were not just higher but also far more confusing:

Prices of seeing the CURIOSITIES.

Lions, each Perſon, - - - - Six-pence.
Foot-Armory, - - - - - Three-pence.
Train of Artillery, - - - - Two-pence.
Horſe-Armory, - - - - - Three-pence.
Spaniſh Armory, - - - - - Two pence.
Regalia, in Company, each Perſon, One Shilling.
——— Single, One Shilling and Six-pence.

N. B. But if a ſingle Perſon is ſhewn the Foot-Armory, Train of Artillery, Horſe-Armory, and *Spaniſh* Armory, he pays for each double the Price above-mentioned.

Apparently this mystifying system did not put many off coming, however, and visitor numbers continued to rise.

But this period of stability did not last long; from the end of the eighteenth century, and the appointment in 1801 of a new keeper, Joseph Bullock, the ever-changing fortunes of the Menagerie began to fail again.* The problem was not only, as it

---

* Incidentally, the previous keeper, whose death created the vacancy that Bullock had been hired to fill, was named George Payne. He was a man remarkable only for being a first cousin of Jane Austen's father.

had been earlier in the century, that the animals were dying particularly quickly, but also that not enough were arriving to meet visitor expectations. Bullock was, as keepers had always been, dependent on chance to keep the Menagerie well stocked – if no foreign monarch or dignitary happened to send the king anything interesting one year, then not a lot could be done about it – the Tower would just have to sit and wait until someone did.

There was only one other possible source of exhibits for the Tower collection. Souvenirs from expeditions of the great explorers had until recently been invaluable for supplementing the collection, providing never-before-seen beasts to keep the Menagerie staff on their toes and the punters happy, but this supply was slowing down too, and quite significantly, by the time of Bullock's appointment. After the burst of activity in the 1760s and 1770s (Captain Cook being the most famous of those embarking on such things at this time), the wars with France and America and the dangers they brought with them meant that costly voyages of discovery were no longer fashionable.

The real hope now came with traders traveling to and from Britain's colonies, primarily those to the east. The East India Company was very active during the 1770s and 1780s, and the constant to-ing and fro-ing of traders meant that for a time the Tower seemed to have a whole fleet of procurers of animals for His Majesty's collection. The inevitable result of this was a shift in the kinds of animals represented in the Tower collection, a sharp bias towards those to be found on the Indian subcontinent – and in a way this served a purpose too, as the collection itself came to symbolize the empire, the strange lands conquered and trophies won. Among them was an elephant presented to the king by the East India Company itself. Then there was the inexplicably named 'shah goest' (which from its picture appears to be a caracal).[*] This particular oddity ('the strange Indian beast,' Horace Walpole called it) had in 1760 been presented by the nabob of Bengal to Robert Clive, who sent it over to William Pitt the Elder, who gave

'The Shah Goest. Drawn from ye Life in ye Tower'; from London Magazine, *December 1759.*

---

[*] Jeremy Osborn and others have suggested that the name is a corrupt derivation of '*siyah-ghush*,' Persian for 'fine ears.' Another possibility is that it is a corruption of 'shawl goat,' an animal the caracal somewhat resembles.

it to the king, who as usual had it placed in the Tower. Not to mention a rhino, antelope, tigers (from Bengal), the strange 'Warwoven' bird described in the children's guidebook; and these were just the ones that survived the journey.

When Captain James Cook set off on his *Endeavour* voyage to the Pacific in 1768, he had on board not just his crew of seamen but a couple of young naturalists as well. One, Dr Daniel Solander, was a friend and student of the eminent Swedish botanist Carolus von Linné (known as Linnaeus). The other, an Englishman like the captain, was a very promising twenty-five-year-old botanist by the name of Joseph Banks. The young Banks (who so impressed Linnaeus that the Swede suggested the newly discovered lands in the Antipodes be named Banksia) would soon be elected president of the Royal Society, a body recently set up in London to promote work in the natural sciences. Banks had requested that he be allowed to accompany the expedition in order to observe and collect botanical samples in the soon-to-be-discovered Pacific islands. And he was not disappointed: he found one Australian bay to be so teeming in exciting plant life that he and the other Englishmen on the *Endeavour* soon dubbed it 'Botany Bay.'

Their investigations of animal life met with rather less success, however. In July 1770 they did sight a hitherto unknown 'kangaroo,' but oddly it seems that no one thought to bring the curious animal back as a gift to His Majesty. Banks's journal for 14 July has a marginal note that reads: 'Kill kanguru.' Which, most efficiently, they did. 'Our second lieutenant who was a shooting today,' writes Banks, 'had the good fortune to kill the animal that had so long been the subject of our speculations.' The journal entry for the following day begins: 'The Beast which was killd yesterday was today Dressd for our dinners and provd excellent meat.' Well, so much for that.

With the precedent set by Banks's trip to Botany Bay in the 1760s, it was soon quite common for naturalists to accompany the voyages of explorers and traders to remote and exotic lands to bring back samples of foreign Nature at her most extraordinary.* (This tradition led, of course, to the invitation extended to Charles Darwin by Robert Fitzroy, the captain of HMS *Beagle*, which in turn led to *The Origin of Species* and all our understanding of the origins, development and variety of life on our planet.) The idea of taking someone onboard to study the flora and fauna discovered across the seas would have been utterly alien to, say, Christopher Columbus, but by the mid–eighteenth century the presence of these men on ships like the *Endeavour* was no more than a reflection

---

* The East India Company itself was taking the natural sciences seriously too. Besides seeking to promote themselves as an enlightened form of government, its members saw the practical benefits of harnessing scientific knowledge for massive potential gain (scientists could help them transplant Chinese tea to India, Himalayan cashmere goats to Scotland, and so on – in the tea market above all, the commercial stakes were very high indeed). Before long the East India Company was funding expeditions, hiring full-time botanists to help with the transportation and transplantation of exotic plants to the Royal Botanic Gardens at Kew and hiring naturalists to keep its traders company on their long sea journeys between home and the empire. The expertise they were buying meant too that it was easier to bring animals back for the king's collection in the Tower, and with Parliament threatening to regulate the Company out of existence the king was now a crucial potential ally.

of a much wider interest back home in England, where natural history was newly seen as a valuable and respectable occupation for a professional, and an admirable pastime for an amateur.*

Questions were being asked, so it was perhaps inevitable that answers would begin to be found. According to an adamant Jeremy Bentham, for example, when one thinks of animals one should ask not 'Can they reason?' or 'Can they talk?' but 'Can they suffer?' (Whether this suffering is understood in terms of God's plan for animals or the workings of a God-independent nervous system – not yet understood – is quite beside the point.)

Across much of northern Europe the particular fashion in the 1750s and 1760s was for describing and ordering (leading ultimately to the exploding of myths, relating to unicorns and such). Dozens of men played a part in this development, ranging from the relatively modest contribution of the Irish-born Oliver Goldsmith (professional writer and amateur naturalist who in 1769 embarked on his *History of the Earth and Animated Nature*) to the crucial work of Linnaeus.

Until the eighteenth century, the classification of species was done according to what would nowadays seem to be quite arbitrary systems. Animals and plants were grouped according to their similarities to each other, whatever form this similarity may take. Some grouped animals by size, or habitat, others by their

---

* Over these same decades, across the Atlantic, the potential power of science had already begun to enthuse great figures like Benjamin Franklin, self-taught Man of the Enlightenment, whose enthusiasm was manifested not in written theory but experiment. The most famous example of this, of course, was his somewhat foolhardy kite-flying experiment of 1752.

usefulness to man. This last was the system preferred by Edward Topsell (the man who described the elephant-sized oxen in chapter 2), who distinguished between those that were useful because they were trustworthy, those that were useful because they were friendly, those that were useful because they were edible, and so on. And until the great Linnaeus developed his classification systems based on species' relations to each other and specifically their reproductive characteristics, a number of those alternative systems suggested bore more than a little resemblance to Borges's parody of a Chinese encyclopaedia (*The Celestial Emporium of Benevolent Knowledge*), which grouped animals into

(a) those that belong to the Emperor, (b) embalmed ones, (c) those that are trained, (d) suckling pigs, (e) mermaids, (f) fabulous ones, (g) stray dogs, (h) those that are included in this classification, (i) those that tremble as if they were mad, (j) innumerable ones, (k) those drawn with a very fine camel's hair brush, (l) others, (m) those that have just broken a flower vase, (n) those that resemble flies from a distance.

It was Linnaeus's publication of his *Species Plantarum* in 1753 and the tenth edition of his *Systema Naturae* (1758) that systematized the naming of plants and animals, respectively, according to genus and species (*Nephrops norvegicus*, *Homarus gammarus*, *Galathea strigosa* or the familiar *Homo sapiens*), the binomial system that is used virtually unchanged today. This meant that all species could at last be sited in a consistent order, with a name that identifies those other species they are related to (those of the same genus – *Homo*, *Homarus*, *Nephrops*, *Galathea*) and gives them a distinguishing epithet too, unique to the species (*sapiens, gammarus, norvegicus, strigosa*). Linnaeus was not entirely without a tendency to moralize when he should have been categorizing (certain animals were 'loathsome,' he said); nonetheless the advances he made were radical ones. By distinguishing sharply between what made a living being and a nonliving one, he played a crucial role in defining the field for life sciences: a study of the world in which man had his place, but suggesting that that place was not at the center. Linnaeus himself would have been surprised at the speed with which so many – even certain churchmen – came to accept his new doctrine.

Linnaeus and his colleagues sparked a fervor of scientific ordering and naming. The fact that it was now (as the children's guidebook showed) that most of the Menagerie's animals were named, for the very first time, is all the more appropriate.

While Linnaeus was overseeing revisions of his *magnum opus* in Uppsala, an equally significant masterwork was being produced in Paris by Georges-Louis Leclerc, the Comte de Buffon. Between 1749 and 1788, the year of his death, Buffon published his seminal *Histoire naturelle, générale et particulière*, which aimed to incorporate all that was known at the time about the natural world into thirty-six magisterial and beautifully illustrated volumes. Buffon was well placed to gather his data; not only was he widely read and educated in botany and medicine (as well as law and mathematics), but since 1739 he had also been the highly esteemed keeper of the royal Jardin des Plantes, indirect successor to Tradescant's old friend and rival Jean Robin (hence the perimeter rue Buffon there today). Buffon didn't hold much with systems like Linnaeus's (nor with any system at all, in truth – he merely classified animals according to their relation to man, in the old style), but he did believe in the virtues of observation and description. Through observation he could assemble facts, and by organizing these facts he could seek to deduce theories to explain them.* As he famously wrote, 'Let us gather facts to give ideas.' Simple, but radical.

Back in England, the layout of the main area of the Menagerie was well suited to the new desire for order, simplicity and tidiness. The arrangement of the cages – a large visitor yard surrounded by a partial ring of cages facing inwards towards the visitor, so there were animals everywhere you looked – follows a model later drawn on by Jeremy Bentham for his Panopticon. This was the prototype for an ideal prison, where a guard could watch all the prisoners from a single spot at the center of the ring (with the implication, according to Foucault, that the power to observe bestows a greater symbolic power on the watcher). The comparison with prisons is not inappropriate, as animals there were neither more nor less than prisoners (neither group with any rights to speak of as yet), and their homes had in the past (remember the Jews in the old elephant house?) been used for humans when prison space had run short. Foucault suggested that Bentham may even have based his idea on the menagerie at Versailles, which had been an octagonal room with an entrance on one side and each of the other seven sides comprising a cage; although Bentham could not have seen the Versailles menagerie, he doubtless would have seen its successor at the Tower. Foucault goes further still: 'The Panopticon is a royal menagerie; the animal is replaced by man.'

---

* Of course, observation per se was nothing new — Aristotle had observed animals when working on his natural history book. Now, however, observation was not limited to the animals' external characteristics and behavior, but focused instead on the workings of the internal anatomy.

The design at the Tower was a typical attempt to impose order on Nature (scientific Nature now, of course, not some kind of responsible theistic creative force) – tidying up the mess left by those first natural historians and their awkward questions.

The new (or newly accurate) interest in specific interrelations between species, between kinds of animals, was also reflected in the Menagerie, manifested in a huge surge in public interest in those animals closest to us. It is only surprising that there are no records of monkeys in the Tower any earlier, since many are known to have been brought to England long before this to be kept as glamorous pets by ladies and gentlemen. Just as primates are and have always been among the great attractions at London Zoo since the early days (the first chimpanzee in Britain was on show at London Zoo from 1835), so the opening in the 1780s of the Menagerie's 'School of Monkeys' caused a sensation. Yet again, here were creatures never before seen by the English public, and yet they were somehow so familiar. It is not surprising that Dr Manette in Dickens's *Tale of Two Cities* (set in this decade) describes the Tower as a place that 'teems with interest.' The entrance fee to the Menagerie had now leveled at about 9d, which Richard Hodgkinson (from Lancashire, in London 'on account of the Lancashire Canal') thought a perfectly reasonable price.

The Monkey Room was laid out not like a prison cell but like a domestic room, a sort of scullery, with shelves and a fireplace, without even bars or barriers separating the visitors and the animals, nothing protecting one from the other. The monkeys were allowed to roam freely around the room, climbing on the visitors, pulling their hair (or more likely, given the prevailing fashion, pulling off their wigs), pinching and biting them. Why should they be kept apart, if they are in fact so like us? A contemporary cartoon depicts a family party visiting the monkeys in the Tower, and the cartoonist, Thomas Rowlandson, makes it quite clear that there is not a great deal to distinguish the people from their animal friends (see plate 13).

The policy of allowing the monkeys freedom of movement within the confines of the visiting room – or, to look at it another way, allowing visitors that freedom in the Monkey Room – did not last long, however, as differences of behavior did manifest themselves, resulting in a certain amount of antagonism. It was this friction that eventually forced the decision that monkeys were more trouble than they were worth; an early nineteenth-century guidebook reports that, yes, '*formerly* several monkeys were kept, but . . . they were removed' (my italics). Apparently one had 'torn a boy's leg in a dangerous manner.' Perhaps they aren't quite as much like us as we first thought.

The second half of the eighteenth century roughly covers the period usually labeled – as a kind of easy shorthand – the Enlightenment. In brief, it was a time characterized by empirical scientific enquiry, and by a recognition of the importance of this enquiry. Certain kinds of curiosity had been frowned on during the Middle Ages and the Renaissance (look at the trouble it had caused Adam and Eve!), but now it pervaded every kind of debate; it would be no exaggeration to say that in these decades a whole new way of looking at the world was born, appearing in great bursts of positivism and creative, intellectual energy.

One of the most significant elements of this, the most significant for our story, at least, was the opening up of a major breach between religion and science. Linnaeus's *Systema Naturae* had interpreted the creations of Nature, but with an understanding that Nature was simply a collection of natural laws that had been *determined by God*. During this subsequent period the link between the two was fundamentally weakened. The gradual secularization of Nature, and the birth of independent science (though still not called 'science' but 'natural philosophy'), became a matter of the most widespread and heated argument with the publication in 1751 of the first edition of Diderot and d'Alembert's *Encyclopédie*, which further polarized science and religion and was roundly condemned by outraged churchmen across the continent.* It was emulated, in England, by the *Encyclopaedia Britannica* in 1771, and so the fervor continued to spread.

The fifteen-year period that began in 1776 with the American Declaration of Independence (itself a revolutionary document of the greatest symbolic significance) was characterized by great writing of the most radical kind – Adam Smith's *Wealth of Nations*, Kant's *Critique of Pure Reason*, Rousseau's *Confessions*, Gibbon's *Decline and Fall of the Roman Empire*, Paine's *Rights of Man* and Mary Wollstonecraft's *Vindication of the Rights of Woman*. By the time this last was completed, James Cook had completed three voyages in the Pacific† (bringing curiosities back with him, living and dead,

---

* It is true that it had traditionally been men of the church who had dabbled in natural philosophy, and they continued to do so throughout this period, but works like the *Encyclopédie* were quite another matter – its scale, its audacity, its scope, its innovativeness were breathtaking and – to some – more than a little threatening.

† To be more precise he only *completed* two of them; he was murdered during the course of the third and his bones were buried in Hawaii.

from Tahiti and elsewhere, to be prodded and tweaked by those back home); the American colonies had won their independence from the oppressive British Crown; and the people of France had stood up in revolution, making great speeches, rising up against their masters, recklessly beheading precious aristocrats as they went. By 1792, four decades after the furor surrounding the *Encyclopédie*, the world could not have been a more different place.

But the fundamental question remained – were animals (and we) created by God or by the seemingly nonarticulated forces of Nature? The question of animals' spirituality and souls was not a straightforward one even for those creationists who were convinced that the answer was the former, and they were rapidly losing ground.

Scientific explanations for life and natural phenomena were well and truly in the ascendant. Even two generations before Darwin's *Origin of Species,* old theories of traditional creationism had begun to be called into question (through Charles's grandfather Erasmus Darwin, Lamarck and others). And studies of the ways of Nature show too what a tiny part man plays in it all. Nothing makes an anthropocentric view of the world harder to sustain than a bit of natural-historical inquisitiveness.

Such newly acquired knowledge not only emphasized how little we did know – throwing our little learning into sharp relief against the vast darknesses as yet uncharted – but served also to excite curiosity still further. And so learning bred learning, and experiment bred experiment, and ways were found of satisfying this thirst for information and experience, for understanding and novelty. And with the development of certain understandings about the workings of nature, as novelties became fewer and further between, so interest began to spread to deviants from this understood norm. We understand sheep and pigs, even lions now, we know how they reproduce, and how they breathe, what and how they eat – but have you ever seen a sheep with five legs? On show today at St George's Inn. See it with your own eyes for just sixpence.

For a time even the Tower tried (rather halfheartedly) to display 'freaks,' starting very early; the *London* Spy in 1700 records seeing 'two preternatural objects, being a dog and a cat, pupped and kittened but with two legs each.' Typically the Spy sees them as no better than 'ill-favoured monsters,' and is more than usually rude to the keeper, who is trying valiantly to explain why the lack of limbs makes them 'highly prized' rather than 'imperfect vermin.' But by the second half of the century the Tower was back on familiar ground – just animals, animals with all the right number of limbs, and with no particular talents to speak of.

Thus Charles Byrne, Hunter's Irish Giant, and other human peculiarities began slowly to pull the public gaze away from the Menagerie. (A lion's a lion, all things considered, and by now we have surely all seen one?) So giants and dwarves, talking pigs and trained bees (yes, really) became the fashion. That was where there was money to be made, and the Tower suddenly found itself with nothing to offer that the public much wanted.

It was not that Bullock was idling in the Tower happily doing nothing; throughout these years he had been trying to improve conditions, repairing the walls of the dens, replacing the rotting wooden grilles with iron ones and so on. But a lack of supply saw the Menagerie's contents dwindle, and no one – neither Bullock nor the constable of the Tower nor the king – made any attempt to remedy this. So as Bullock sat in the Tower waiting, vainly cleaning and improving and modernizing, the collection began to disintegrate. And inevitably the ageing keeper began to lose heart.

One indicator of the Menagerie's failing fortunes and flagging public interest in it can be found by looking into its coverage in the press, and the drop in incidences is striking. Where, for example, in 1792 Menagerie stories had featured in the *Times* on no less than four occasions in under eight months, during Bullock's twenty-one-year tenure it was not considered worthy of one single mention.

In 1809 there was still a sizeable collection, though probably not a particularly happy or healthy one. A guidebook that year describes all those things one might expect to find there: an old

'Fanny Howe, whelp'd in the Tower': a 1794 engraving of a Tower lioness, one of the public's favorites.

195

lioness (Miss Fanny) bred in the Tower, lions and lionesses brought from Persia, Morocco and Algeria, tigers (which had killed eight slaves as they attempted to evade capture), a Barbary panther called Traveller, a black leopardess called Miss Peggy ('her spots are very visible, though black'), a hyena, a wolf from Mexico, a white fox, a raccoon, a jackal, an 'Eagle of the Sun' and more.

By 1815 the collection had already begun to dwindle significantly. Besides the lions, all it contained was 'one panther, one hyena, one tigress, one jackall, one mountain cow and one large bear.' Of this sorry crew, the highlight, which did redeem things somewhat, and which kept a small but steady stream of visitors coming to the Tower to pay their respects, was Old Martin.

Old Martin was a great grizzly bear from America, a gift to George III from the Hudson Bay Company, and the first grizzly seen in England. He had arrived in 1811, and by the late 1820s was one of the Menagerie's longest-standing residents.

> The name of Martin, which was originally bestowed on him,
> in imitation probably of that of the most celebrated bear ever
> exhibited in Europe, has consequently been of late years
> generally preceded by the epithet of antiquity, and Old
> Martin has become under that title almost as well known as
> his famous namesake.

Old Martin was a very large, very fierce beast indeed (his ferocity not softened by his age, to the surprise of many). The guidebook continues:

He does not offer the slightest encouragement to familiarity on the part of his keepers, but treats them with as much distance as the most perfect strangers; and although he will sometimes appear playful and good tempered, yet they know him too well to trust themselves within his clutch.

The public, of course, didn't have to worry about Martin (the dangerous jobs were left to the keepers). Quite the reverse, in fact; the greater the potential for ferocity, the bigger the thrill.

In spite of Old Martin and his apparently endless ability to charm his public, and in spite of Bullock's attempts at improvement, it seemed that no one could stop the creeping sense of discouragement and decay. Morale at the Menagerie must surely have been at an all-

Visiting the Tower Menagerie, c. 1820.

time low, and this can only have contributed towards conditions being allowed to slip, just slightly, especially during the prolonged Napoleonic Wars, only lately ended. Someone had to find some way of raising numbers, not only visitor numbers, which were falling steadily in a competitive market, but the number of animals.

And those few that there were might die at any moment, for conditions in the Tower were still very poor. It was less crowded now, yes, but only because the mortality rate was so high, which is hardly a recommendation; and the public mood was veering more and more towards compassion and a pragmatic consideration of animals. Scientists and preachers alike were coming around to the idea that they were not as absolutely different from us as Renaissance Londoners had believed. Scientists and their Enlightened followers recognized animals' capacity for suffering, and preachers recognized that they had been created – like us – by God and were therefore eligible for divine protection and possibly even salvation too. Neither party was happy with the way Bullock's stragglers were living. Never before had the concept of animals' rights taken any firm hold of the public's attention, but now it began to do so with furious enthusiasm.

At the Menagerie something drastic had to be done. If just two more animals died, there'd be nothing left but birds. The death in 1822 of the keeper, the well-intentioned but sadly ineffectual Joseph Bullock, made that something possible.

8

Compassion and Competition, and the Last Days of the Menagerie

The highlight of the 1811 Christmas season at Covent Garden was the appearance on stage of the great Chunee. He was making his theatrical debut in pantomime – in *Harlequin and Padmanaba*, to be precise – and his performance was highly acclaimed (a good thing, as the theatre manager Henry Harris had had to pay 900 guineas for his appearance). The fact that he turned out to be unable to discharge his part very thoroughly seemed immaterial to his fans, who assumed either that 'he had indulged too freely in his cups' or that 'the tremendous noise of his reception deprived him of *sense* and *recollection*.'

Chuneelah, known as 'Chunee' to his adoring public, was a six-year-old Indian elephant, who since 1810 had been on show at

Edward Cross's successful Exeter 'Change Menagerie just off the Strand, where today Burleigh Street crosses Exeter Street, running down to the Lyceum Theatre from Covent Garden market. Like Jumbo at London Zoo in 1882, or Chi-Chi the giant panda in the 1950s, Chunee was a national darling, a celebrity, the events in his (admittedly rather uneventful) life reported in the press, the serious press, as if he were royalty.

Chunee had everything. He had fame, public adoration, regular and generous feedings, and even a forty-night West End run to his name. What more could an elephant ask for?

There was, it turns out, just one thing missing from his comfortable life. Reports of the day describe (ever so delicately) how for a few years Chunee had been going through regular (annual) cycles of aggression, but they don't suggest (though it must have been as clear to them as it is to us) what it was that he wanted – the same thing all male elephants want at that age.

Chunee had gained a reputation for having a temper (though only in season of course) – this had been unheard of in his earliest days in London, but common in the past five or six years ('strong symptoms of irritability during a certain season'). He was not the first and certainly not the last to let his temper get the better of him on the Covent Garden stage – one can almost imagine him throwing a tantrum and storming offstage to his dressing room in a rage – but it didn't seem to be getting any better. The real unraveling began back at Exeter 'Change on Sunday, 26 February 1826; his moods were getting worse, and he had taken to throwing himself around his den so forcefully that a part of the room had been destroyed, and 'such was the ferocity of the elephant, that the carpenters were unable to repair it.' This was all the more serious because the Exeter 'Change Menagerie was installed on the second floor of the building, a floor that was not built to hold five-ton elephants. The floor of Chunee's own cell had been specially reinforced, but the rest of the Menagerie's rooms had not. If in one of his rages Chunee managed to break out of his cell, he risked crashing straight through the floor to the parade of shops below, taking the whole Menagerie with him.

The entrance to the Exeter 'Change Menagerie, seen in 1829 just before it was finally pulled down.

Cross had no choice but to take drastic action. It was Wednesday, 1 March 1826.

Mr Cross at once determined on having him destroyed, and after some consideration as to the mode in which this should be effected, it was resolved to give him a quantity of corrosive sublimate in a mess of hay. The sagacity of the animal was, however, proof against this attempt, for he no sooner smelt the mixture than he rejected it, and it was therefore determined to shoot him. Accordingly a messenger was sent to Somerset-house, where two soldiers, as usual, were on guard, who, on a suitable representation being made, were allowed to go over to the Menagerie, taking with them their muskets. Several rifle-guns were also obtained from different places in the neighbourhood, and put into the hands of such of the persons about the establishment as had courage enough to remain in the room – In this manner, in all about fourteen persons were armed. . . .

The muskets loaded, about a third of the party advanced to the front of the den, till within about five yards of the animal, and discharged their pieces at the tender part of the neck below the ear, and then immediately retreated to a recess at the lower end of the room for the purposes of reloading. The animal, on finding himself wounded, uttered a loud and piercing groan; and, advancing to the front of the den, struck his trunk several times with all his fury against the bars. . . .

Having in this manner at last exhausted his fury, he became quiet, upon which another detachment of the party approached his den, and after firing on him, retired into the recess as before. The animal, on receiving the fire, again plunged most furiously against the front of the den, the door of which he actually lifted from off its uppermost hinge, but was prevented from getting out by the strong manner in which the ropes bound the different bars together. On his becoming more tranquil, preparations were made for firing another volley, but no sooner were the muskets about to be levelled, than the animal, as if conscious of their being the cause of his wounds, and also of the vulnerable parts against which they were intended to be directed, turned sharp round and retreated into the back of the den, and hid his head between his shoulders. It in consequence became necessary to rouse him, by pricking him with spears, which being effected, the muskets were discharged at him, and although several balls evidently took effect in the neck on this as well as on former occasions, still he did not exhibit any signs of weakness, beyond abstaining from those violent efforts, which he had previously made against the front of his den: indeed, from this time he kept almost entirely at the back of his den, and although the blood flowed profusely from the wounds he had received, he gave no other symptom of passion or pain, than an occasional groan or kick against the side of the den. For almost an hour and a half in this manner, a continued discharge of musketry was kept up against him, and no less than 152 bullets were expended before he fell to the ground, where he lay motionless, and was soon dispatched with a sword which, after being secured on the end of a rifle, was plunged into his neck. The quantity of blood that flowed from him was very considerable, and flooded the den to a considerable depth.

Another account, rather more sympathetic, chose to conclude the sad story thus: 'The noble brute seated himself on his haunches, then folded his forelegs under him, adjusted his trunk and ceased to live, the only peaceful one among us cruel wretches.'

A cannon had been called for, but fortunately there was no call to use it. Chunee was dead, at last. There was silence for the briefest moment, hardly a minute's respectful pause, and then the room was opened again, for the public to come in and see the spoils of the massacre – the great, beloved elephant lying in a huge pool of blood, still chained by the back legs to one of the cell walls. The usual admission price applied, of course – 1s 6d. Demand was so great (visitors to the site of the massacre that night included the bishop of London and Humphry Davy, Banks's successor as president of the Royal Society) that Cross kept the spectacle open extra-late that night.

Chunee was passed into the hands of a team of scientists, who saw him as a dissection opportunity not to be missed. He was flayed and cut up, examined, prodded and weighed, and a full coroner's report was written. His skin was sold for £50, the rest of his bulk sold as eleven thousand pounds of meat (everything except the two large steaks that those conducting the experiments on the Sunday 'cut from the rump of the elephant, and cooked'). Chunee's skeleton was transported to the Hunterian Museum, where it remained on display for over a century, finally succumbing to wartime damage.

It comes as no surprise that there was a public outcry over the manner of dispatching this poor creature, but there was also (and more interestingly) an outcry over the way he had been kept in captivity. There were poems written, broadsides published, gruesome pictures printed showing an 'Exact Representation of the Manner of DESTROYING THE ELEPHANT' (see, for example, plate 14). *The Times* carried numerous stories – following what happened to the body over the succeeding week or so – culminating in a letter to the editor that appeared on Friday, 10 March.

Sir, I observe in this day's *Times*, two letters denying that their writers had either eaten, or caused to be eaten, elephant rump-stakes; and I am quite ready to acknowledge their gastric delicacy, though I can say nothing for their humanity or taste, as they take no notice of the total want of both in English Menageries.

To place an elephant, or any beast, without a mate, in a box bearing no greater proportion to his bulk than a coffin does to a corpse, is inhuman; and there can be no doubt that confinement and the want of a mate caused the frenzy which rendered it necessary to destroy the late stupendous and interesting animal at Exeter 'Change.

In France, you know, Sir, the Jardin des Plantes contains a Menagerie at once humane, safe, and a national ornament. . . . An appendage of a royal court should surely be worthy of a monarch. Conceive the feelings of a Frenchman, after paying to see our national establishment at the Tower, and comparing it with the truly royal one at Paris, which all the world can see gratis.

I am, Sir, your obedient servant,
CHUNY

Principled people with ideas like this were bound to cause real trouble for the Tower Menagerie, sooner or later.

But meanwhile, back on stage: before the year was out Sadler's Wells was doing excellent business with its new tragedy: *Chuneelah, or The Death of the Elephant at Exeter 'Change.*

But in 1822 Chunee was still alive and popular, with few hints of the dangerous behavior that was soon to bring his downfall. The man largely responsible for Chunee's success was his keeper, Alfred Cops, who had taught him the tricks that had so impressed his visitors – numbering among them Queen Victoria (the Princess Victoria, as she was then), a teenage Charles Dickens, and Lord Byron, who on a visit in November 1813 joked he'd have liked to have employed Chunee as his butler! Cops was a professional zoologist and an expert on animal behavior, a man with extensive training and experience looking after captive animals. As such he was an obvious choice to take over Joseph Bullock's duties in the Tower after Bullock's death. It was expected that such a man would be able to expand and improve the Menagerie, making it exciting and competitive in a way it had not been for some years, and at the same time improve the animals' living conditions sufficiently to satisfy the newly fashionable anticruelty lobbies.

From the moment he took up his post in 1822, Cops threw himself energetically and enthusiastically into what must have seemed a daunting task. Bullock's twenty-one years of neglect (albeit unintentional) had left the collection in a pitiful state, and by the time of Cops's appointment it contained just 'an elephant, a brown bear' (the much-loved Old Martin, of course) and 'a bird or two.' But the King, George IV, was fascinated by things exotic and had aspirations for greater glories for his Menagerie. And Cops himself was determined that under his stewardship London would again have a Royal Menagerie whose popularity surpassed all other sights of the city, fully stocked with an unprecedented range of exotic – but also happy and comfortable – animals of all shapes and sizes. His wish was realized, for a time.

Unlike any of his predecessors, Cops was not prepared to rely on chance gifts to the king or souvenirs from explorers for stocking his collection. Like the Tradescants two centuries earlier, Cops saw his role partly as that of an active procurer of specimens. He would go out into the wide world to find them out there, if necessary; he would negotiate with other collectors, and with travelers and seamen, with dealers and dockworkers; and above all he would be prepared to spend a great deal of money (this may have been the part the king didn't like quite as much), investing in the collection itself and in its ongoing welfare. In the words of one poster advertizing the Menagerie's delights, 'The highest Prices given for every kind of Foreign Beast & Birds.' Besides looking after the royal animals, Cops was a collector himself, and exhibited his own animals at the Tower alongside the king's (much as Jean Robin had done with his own plants at Louis XIII's Jardin des Plantes two centuries earlier), which also helped to keep animal numbers up.

For the first time in the Menagerie's six-hundred-year history the animals in the Tower were under the supervision not of some retired soldier or official honored with the Tower sinecure (and finding that the Menagerie took up rather a lot of his large port-folio there) but of a trained animal man – and it showed. Cops asked crucial questions, obvious questions, it may seem now, but nonetheless questions entirely neglected by his predecessors. What should we be feeding them? Do they have enough space? How are these species related to each other, if at all? The result of his inter-est and enthusiasm was a Menagerie that by 1828 had grown from the lamentable Regency collection to include over sixty different species, and a total of nearly three hundred animals. By 1830, when John Bayley wrote his *History and Antiquities of the Tower of London*, Cops's 'spirited exertions, without regard to trouble or expense, [had] rendered it one of the finest collections in the universe.'

In his first few years on the job, Cops oversaw a major restruc-turing of the Menagerie, including improvements to the existing cages and the constructing of new homes for the new species he intended to acquire. One of the most significant changes Cops was responsible for was the erection of a large building to serve as a combined aviary and small animal house. Completed around 1827, this building was some 40 feet long, quite a considerable size in the already cramped Menagerie area.

One effect of this improvement in the conditions in which ani-mals were kept was that happier creatures seemed more prepared to breed, many doing so for the first time. The pelicans from Hungary nested, for what was probably the first time in captivity; a python laid eggs (though alas failed to incubate them) and so on.

Memorials of the Tower of London, published in 1830, described the layout:

[The animals] are confined in two yards, in a double tier of dens, strongly barred, except those requiring greater warmth, which are kept within doors. In the first yard, the dens are disposed in a semi-circular building, which, although now faced with brick, and otherwise altered, is apparently a remain of an ancient Tower, the back wall being at least seven feet in thickness. About three years ago, Mr. Cops erected a large room, seventy [*sic*] feet in length (in place of some stabling, &c.,) for the birds and graminivorous animals. The carnivorous beasts are mostly kept in the dens of the outer-yard.

The organization was unprecedented.

In 1829, the naturalist Edward T. Bennett had published *The Tower Menagerie*, a sort of exhibition catalogue describing and illustrating the Menagerie's holdings at that time. In his introduction, he writes:

Of the animals contained in [the collection] during the summer of 1828, and of two others which had then recently died, the succeeding pages offer delineations, descriptions, and anecdotes . . . so excellent is the management of Mr Cops, especially as regards cleanliness, that essential security of animal health, that not a single death has occurred from disease, and only one from an accidental cause. . . . As a visit to the Menagerie will enable the reader at once to compare our representations and descriptions with their living prototypes, the imperative necessity of scrupulous accuracy has been deeply impressed throughout the whole undertaking on the minds of those who have been engaged in its completion.

The contents page of Bennett's catalogue reads as follows; note how (in most cases) the animals have been grouped together sensibly – mammals with mammals (felines together, simians together, etc.), reptiles with reptiles, birds with birds and so on. Bennett starts with the big cats, always the biggest draw:

Bengal Lion
Lioness and Cubs
Cape Lion
Barbary Lioness
Tiger
Leopard
Jaguar
Puma
Ocelot
Caracal [the 'shah goest,' as it had once been known]
Chetah, or Hunting Leopard
Striped Hyaena
Hyaena-Dog
Spotted Hyaena
African Bloodhound
Wolf
Clouded Black Wolf
Jackal
Civet, or Musk Cat
Javanese Civet

Gray Ichneumon

Paradoxurus

Brown Coati

Racoon

American Black Bear

Grizzly Bear

Thibet Bear

Bornean Bear

Egret Monkey

Common Macaque

Bonneted Monkey

Pig-faced Baboon

White-headed Mongoos

Kanguroo

Porcupine

Asiatic Elephant [possibly the nabob of Arcot's]

Zebra of the Plains

Llama

Rusa-Deer

Indian Antelope

African Sheep

Golden Eagle

Great Sea-Eagle

Bearded Griffin

Griffon Vulture

Secretary

Virginian Horned Owl

Deep-blue Macaw

Blue and Yellow Macaw

Yellow-crested Cockatoo
New Holland Emeu
Crested Crane
Pelican
Alligator
Indian Boa
Anaconda
Rattlesnake

Each animal, besides a description of its nature (often anecdotal) and its origins, has a portrait done from the life.

The whole of the drawings are from the pencil of MR WILLIAM HARVEY, who, in seizing faithful and characteristic portraits of animals in restless and almost incessant motion, has succeeded in overcoming difficulties which can only be appreciated by those who have attempted similar delineations.

And as though to emphasize the importance of naturalism and accuracy in these pictures,

the engravings have been executed throughout by MESSRS BRANSTON and WRIGHT. Determined on securing the accuracy of the representations, they have in every instance compared the proofs with the animals, and have made corrections where necessary until the resemblance has been rendered perfect.

Producing another animal catalogue the following year, Bennett admits that the classification system he uses in his books is itself not yet perfect, owing to a lack of access on his part to the latest work on the subject:

> The Editor hoped too that before the conclusion of a
> volume he should be enabled to arrange the Quadrupeds in
> a series more strictly consonant with their natural affinities
> than any that has hitherto been proposed. But his own
> views on the subject are not sufficiently matured for
> publication; and those of his friend MR VIGORS, which
> the zoological world are anxiously expecting, have not yet
> appeared.

This is not ideal, then, but by drawing attention to it Bennett shows himself aware of the discussions in this subject (if not actually fully familiar with them), and aware too that such things matter.

Where previous guides to the Menagerie were very visitor-centered, only bothering to treat the collection's more glamorous highlights, Bennett's book looked equally at all species (even giving their two-part Latin names), and made some attempt to relate each to the others.

> In his moral and intellectual faculties, as well as in his
> external and physical characters, the Lion exhibits a close
> agreement with the strikingly distinct and well marked
> group to which he belongs, and of which he is
> unquestionably the first in rank and importance: and perhaps

the most effectual means of guarding against the general
prejudice, which has delighted in exalting him at the expense
of his fellow beasts, will be found in the recollection that,
both physically and morally, he is neither more nor less than
a cat, of immense size and corresponding power it is true,
but not on that account the less endowed with all the guileful
and vindictive passions of that faithless tribe.

Or here, describing the porcupine:

Although the Rodent order, next to the Carnivorous, is the
most numerous in species, the Porcupine is the only animal
belonging to it which is at present contained in the Menagerie.
The animals of this division, consisting chiefly of 'rats and mice
and such small deer,' have indeed, with some few exceptions,
so little of interest for the mere casual visiter of an exhibition,
that it is rarely that they are sought after unless by the scientific
collector. They are at once distinguished from the Carnivora
by the total absence of canine teeth.

The fact that Bennett is a most conscientious and egalitarian
recorder – including in his catalogue not just those animals popular with the public, or just those of which he is personally fond,
but dealing with each in the collection in some detail and at some
length – does not mean to say, however, that he is not partisan,
that he doesn't make his own tastes known; quite the reverse, he
has strong views about those animals he approves of and those he
doesn't, and his tastes can be surprising. Although primates had
been among the more popular attractions of the Tower Menagerie

as long as they had been in the collection, Bennett is very dismissive of them and their 'so much vaunted intelligence' (he personally believes them to be too stupid to train, and 'barbarous'). The baboon, for instance, is 'stupid and savage'; his 'gross brutality is scarcely relieved by a single spark of intelligence.' But while refusing to recognize a kinship with his 'monkeys' group he is quite prepared to ascribe humanlike feelings to (and recognize pseudohuman behavior in) many other animals in the collection.

Look, for instance, at the pair of Bengal tigers. This is the male, brought over on an East India Company boat:

> On the voyage he was remarkably tame, allowing the sailors
> to play with him, and appearing to take much pleasure in
> their caresses. On being placed in his present den he was
> rather sulky for a few days; but seems now to have recovered
> his good temper, and to be perfectly reconciled to his
> situation.*

The female was equally unhappy to be transferred into the keeping of Mr Cops.

> Her deportment was so sulky and savage that Mr Cops could
> scarcely be prevailed on by her former keeper, who saw her

---

* Incidentally, Bennett ascribes the animal's good nature to the fact that in his early years he was never allowed to eat meat. In the Menagerie he is now fed meat, which 'he seems particularly to enjoy, although he has by no means lost his appetite for soup, which he devours with much eagerness.'

shortly afterwards, to allow him to enter her den: but no sooner did she recognise her old friend, than she fawned on him, licked him, and caressed him, exhibiting the most extravagant signs of pleasure; and when he left her she cried and whined for the remainder of the day. To her new residence and her new keeper she is now perfectly resigned.

From what we read in Bennett, then, it would sound as though these two tigers were not immediately impressed by the conditions in the Tower Menagerie; but they would have been far more dismayed at the conditions in which they would have been kept had they had the misfortune to have been brought to the Tower a couple of centuries earlier – like the tiger Thomas Platter described seeing in 1599, for example. For although today we would balk at keeping captive animals in nineteenth-century conditions, they were indescribably better than they had been those few centuries earlier. Cops was dedicated to improving not only the visitors' experience but also the animals' experience, and the changes he wrought did indeed effect a marked improvement, and a much-needed one, in their standard of living.

Cops's innovative aviary and small mammal and reptile house (whose snakes were apparently 'kept warmly wrapped up in blankets over a stove, and after making a dinner on fowls and rabbits, they take a siesta of three weeks or a month's duration') provided a space for displaying those animals that were not immediately seen as grand or attractive to the public (as the elephants, big cats or bears had always been) but were nonetheless worth having for reasons of scientific curiosity. Meanwhile, to keep the visitors interested, other innovations were introduced – among them was the zebra,* who wasn't caged but was instead ridden around the yard by a young boy and occasionally rewarded for his good behavior with a sip of ale. The lion cubs were allowed to run free too, for visitors to pet, as Saussure had done a hundred years earlier. Even the jaguar was 'so mild as to lick the hands of visitors.'

The living arrangements could still have been better, of course; too often antagonistic animals were unthinkingly placed danger-ously close to one another. One unfortunate secretary bird, 'having incautiously introduced its long neck into the den of the hyena, was deprived of it and of its head at one bite.' One hyena there, probably the same one, shared his 'den' with an American black bear, and while neither actually succeeded in killing the other, relations between the roommates were hardly harmonious, for they were prone to fight 'in a very ludicrous manner, for a piece of beef, or whatever else might happen to furnish a bone of contention between them.' In these disputes it was the devious hyena who usually had the last laugh.

The most notorious encounter of this kind came on 3 December 1830, when one of Cops's assistants carelessly left open a door between the lion enclosure and the den containing

---

* The appearance of this first zebra begs the (trivial, but interesting) question: what reference point did children's alphabet books use for the letter Z before the appearance of 'Z is for Zebra' (or indeed 'Z is for Zoo')? The answer is reveal-ing: if 'A is for Apple' and 'B is for Book' (or Ball, or Bear), then apparently 'Z is for Zealot.' Quite how this might have been explained to a child of pre–reading age I'm not entirely sure.

Bennett's moody Bengal tiger and tigress. Within moments they were engaged in the fiercest struggle, which lasted quite some time, with even the most energetic efforts on the part of the desperate keepers unable to stop them. The tigers, with the advantage of numbers, largely had control of the fight, and though they were finally separated from their victim after a half-hour mauling, by heated brands held to their nostrils and mouths, the injured lion did not survive more than a few days. Poor Mr Cops was distraught, as were the other animals, who were worked into a state of alarm at the noise: 'The roaring and yelling of the combatants resounded through the yards, and excited in the various animals the most lively demonstrations of fear and rage. The smaller and the pacific tribes shivered with dread.'

Word of this fight spread quickly across the city – numerous illustrations were made, reports appeared in the press. But the precept that 'all publicity is good publicity' notwithstanding, murmur of this particular episode did the Menagerie's reputation no good at all. It was a considerable public embarrassment. Apparently the devoted Mr Cops was not the only one who found it distressing (though not so long ago they would have sold tickets for such a fight).

But for all these problems things could have been far worse. The animals did at least have a keeper who was interested in them and absolutely dedicated to their welfare, even to the point where he often found himself at considerable risk, on one occasion almost going the way of his old secretary bird. He was holding the head of a huge constrictor snake to which he was about to feed a bird of some kind, when, as the *Times* reported:

the snake darted at the bird, missed it, but seized the keeper by the thumb, and was coiled around his arm and neck in a moment. Mr Cops, who was alone, did not lose his presence of mind, and immediately attempted to relieve himself from the powerful constrictor, by pulling at its head: but it had so knotted itself upon its own head, Mr Cops could not reach it, and had thrown himself upon the floor, in order to grapple with a better chance of success, when two other keepers coming in, they broke the teeth of the serpent, and with some difficulty relieved Mr Cops from the fate of Laocoon, which might otherwise have been his also.*

Clearly the devoted Alfred Cops did not insist on being an arm's-length keeper, as most of his predecessors had been. It is hard to imagine old William de Botton letting himself get into this kind of trouble.

The boa wasn't the only troublemaker. There was one leopard who

evinced a particular predilection for the destruction of umbrellas, parasolls, muffs, hats, and such other articles of dress as may happen to come within her reach, seizing them with the greatest quickness and tearing them into pieces almost before the astonished visitor has become aware of the loss.

---

* The moral of the story? 'It may not be amiss to give persons who have the care of BOA CONSTRICTORS a hint not to expose their hands too much in holding fowls, &c., to the head of a Boa, when near shedding its skin and consequently nearly blind.'

According to Bennett, 'Mr Cops declares he has no doubt that during her residence in the Tower she has made prey of at least as many of these articles as there are days in the year.'

Leaving such chaos aside, in purely statistical terms the Menagerie had never seen such success. The public were more than ever before aware of its existence and the goings-on in it (and not just the fights). It appeared frequently in the national press, with stories and advertisements a regular feature. The need to advertise also meant that the Menagerie had to think of ways of making the visitor experience appear more attractive, and so the advertisements would commonly include special draws such as the promise of watching 'feeding time,' which would be an exciting and reasonably safe way of observing the wilder behavior of these animals spill out for a few minutes. Such advertising worked, and visitor numbers reached an unprecedented high.

The nation couldn't have been prouder. Even the *Times*, hardly prone to overexcitement, gushed in 1827:

> Few objects are calculated to throw a greater lustre on our national character, in an emulative point of view, than the splendid specimens of savage nature which the resources of Government have succeeded in collecting. Birds, beasts, reptiles, in endless variety, press on the spectator's view and lead him through the labyrinth with wonderment superior to any before exhibited.

The Tower Menagerie seemed at last to have found its place. If Cops was to keep visitor figures high, however, the occasional piece of advertising was not enough. He had already greatly

The KING'S  Menagerie ROYAL

Tower of London.

This ancient Edifice, built in the reign of Edward IV. 1465, for the reception of FOREIGN

BEAST, BIRDS, &c.

Presented to the Kings of England, could never, since its foundation, boast of a more magnificent and splendid VARIETY than it does at present.

First Department.—A beautiful majestic full-grown

BENGAL LION

AND HIS CONSORT, IN ONE DEN,

Being the largest that has been brought to England for many years, and presented to the King by General Watson; the only pair of this kind ever seen in this Country.—FOUR beautiful

AFRICAN LIONS in one Den.—Pair of beautiful

YOUNG LIONS

From the Cape of Good Hope.—Pair of beautiful BENGAL

ROYAL TIGERS

Just Landed, the first that has been in the Menagerie for 20 years.—Pair of

Oriental LEOPARDS, remarkable for docility.---Beautiful PANTHER.

THE STRIPED or UNTAMEABLE HYÆNA,

Beautiful AFRICAN

Leopard & her Cubs

Pair of Spotted or LAUGHING HYÆNAS.--Pair of enormous Black WOLVES

From the Polar Regions; the only ones ever seen alive in England.

PAIR OF ORIENTAL PORCUPINES,

Whose power of raising or depressing their quills renders them so formidable to their pursuers.

Three African BLOOD-HOUNDS.—An enormous GRIZLY BEAR from Hudson's Bay.

WHOSE BULK EXCEEDS THAT OF AN OX.

A fine BLACK BEAR from North America.---A remarkably beautiful

OCELOT, OR TIGER CAT.

This animal creates universal admiration.—The CIVET-CAT, the animal that produces Musk.

COATI MONDIES or Ant-eaters, RACOONS,

With an infinite variety of SIMIA, or MONKEY Tribe, whose antics and gambols afford the highest amusement.

Second Department.

A Beautiful Zebra,

From Ethiopia.

A BEAUTIFUL MALE NYLGHAU,

From the Coromandel Coast.—A PAIR OF

KANGAROOS,

(Male & Female) Bred in Windsor Great Park.

The MOUFFLON, from Caffraria.—4 EMEWS or

SOUTHERN OSTRICHES.

Three extraordinary fine

PELICANS of the WILDERNESS,

Represented to feed their Young with their own Blood.

ARDEA DUBIA,

Or ADJUTANT of BENGAL, commonly called the Gigantic Crane.

Belearic or Royal Crowned Cranes.—Cyrus or Polish Crane.

Hooded VULTURE from China, & a Bearded VULTURE or GRIFFIN.—Majestic

EAGLE of the SUN

And Golden Eagle,

FROM NORTH AMERICA.

Pair of beautiful Horned Owls, from Hudson's Bay; Pair of Storks, from Elsineur; Pair of Spoon-bills, from Holland.

TWO PAIR OF CURACOA BIRDS, FROM TRINIDAD.

Majestic Elk, from the East Indies.

Chinese Gold and Silver Pheasants, Macaws, Cockatoos, Parrots, Paroquets, and a great variety of other Birds of the most splendid plumage.

The Tapier or Hippopotamus of South America.

Boa Constrictors, or Great Serpents of Jaba,

The largest ever exhibited.

The ANACONDA SNAKE, next in magnitude to the above.

The Beasts are regularly FED at 3 in the Afternoon, which will be found the most interesting time. NO EXTRA CHARGE.
N. B. The highest Price given for every kind of Foreign Beasts & Birds.

Admittance, only 1s. to view the whole Menagerie.

WHEELER, Printer, 21, Bermondsey St.

improved conditions, though not perhaps enough for some, and he would have to do so still further; most important, he knew he would have to keep his collection well stocked with more animals and species if he was to have any chance of combating the large and growing threat of competition.

There was Exeter 'Change, of course, until 1826 home to Chunee among other fine specimens, which had grown in success and fame since the end of the previous century, as the Tower Menagerie had declined; but this was by no means the only threat. By now London had acquired dozens of other attractions too; so it housed not just animal collections and freak shows, but grand exhibitions offering visitors all kinds of experience, some more edifying than others. The first quarter of this new century saw the public display of great collections like the National Gallery, in a house on Pall Mall, and the arrival from France of Madame Tussaud and her famous waxworks. Besides these were the public fairs, each with any number of strange sights. Writing about his residence in London, Wordsworth recalled:

> All moveables of wonder from all parts
> Are here, albinos, painted Indians, dwarfs,
> The horse of knowledge, and the learned pig,
> The stone-eater, the man that swallows fire,
> Giants, ventriloquists, the invisible girl,
> The bust that speaks and moves its goggling eyes,
> The waxwork, clockwork, all the marvellous craft
> Of modern Merlins, wild beasts, puppet-shows,
> All out-o'-th'-way, far-fetched, perverted things,
> All freaks of Nature, all Promethean thoughts

Of man – his dulness, madness, and their feats,
All jumbled up together to make up
This parliament of monsters.

And besides all these London-based sights there were the traveling shows, boasting animals as magnificent as any more permanent collection. Indeed, the large Exeter 'Change rooms had originally been opened by Gilbert Pidcock as a place to house only his own traveling show during its months at home. The pioneer in this area was George Wombwell, who had set up the very first traveling menagerie (his 'Royal Menagerie,' as he called it) in 1810, and continued to take his animals on the road, to small towns the length and breadth of the country, for several decades. Tigers, elephants, rhinos and polar bears were just some of the animals he exhibited over the years. His tomb in Highgate, with a striking statue of a lion lying atop it, calls him simply a 'Menagerist.'

There seemed to be no limit to the London public's taste for such spectacles. As early as 1773 a catalogue of London sights had boasted (albeit with some exaggeration) that there were 'Lions, Tygers, Elephants, &c. in every Street in Town.'

Conditions in many of these places were appalling, however, even by the more modest standards of the 1820s, and for the first time this was not to be tolerated.

Let us go back a little, to the year 1822, the year when Alfred Cops's appointment to the Tower post had just been announced. The anticruelty lobby had grown in size rapidly over the preceding two or three years, and had also become far more vocal. The public mood was recognized with the passing of the first animal-cruelty legislation, the Animal Protection Act, which outlawed mistreatment of cattle, sheep and horses, and was steered through Parliament by Richard Martin MP. There had of course been previous prohibitions on activities like bear-baiting, as in the days of Oliver Cromwell, but these had not sought to prevent cruelty to animals, but to limit social vices – protection of animals had been just an accidental side-effect.

Another two years saw the establishment of the world's first animal welfare organization, the Society for the Prevention of Cruelty to Animals (the SPCA – more familiar, since the granting of Queen Victoria's charter in 1840, as the RSPCA), whose sole purpose was to defend animal rights and prosecute anyone infringing those rights.[*] Those in attendance at the Society's first meeting in a coffee house on St Martin's Lane included Richard Martin and William Wilberforce MP, till lately an ardent campaigner for the abolition of slavery. The minutes of this first meeting describe a 'Society instituted for the purpose of preventing cruelty to animals.'

It was resolved:

—That a committee be appointed to superintend the Publication of Tracts, Sermons, and similar modes of influencing public opinion. . . .

---

[*] They secured 149 convictions for cruelty in their first year alone, a surprisingly high figure bearing in mind that this was not only the first animal welfare organization in the world, but also Britain's first law-enforcement agency of any kind, preceding even the Metropolitan police force by five years.

Bartholomew Fair.

THE Greatest Wonder in England IS

CATS! THE LEARNED

SIGNOR CAPPELLI

(Previous to his leaving London) begs leave most respectfully to inform the Visitors and Inhabitants of the Metropolis, that having met the most flattering encouragement while in Regent-street, London, Brighton, Bath, Cheltenham, Manchester, Liverpool, Dublin, Edinburgh, &c. &c. where he has been patronised by the Nobility and Gentry, will now exhibit his WONDERFUL AMUSEMENTS,

Performed by Cats,
At 19, GILTSPUR STREET,
EVERY DAY
DURING THE FAIR.

The Entertainment will commence with an Exhibition of some extraordinary manoeuvres or

SLEIGHT of HAND
By Signor Cappelli, the Inimitable Tuscan;

Executed in a style the most remarkable and unknown in the country. The Cats will then be introduced, and their performance will be, ts beat a drum, turn a spit, grind knives, play music, strike upon an anvil, roast coffee, ring bells, set a piece of machinery in motion to grind rice in the Italian manner, with many other astonishing exercises. One of the Cats, the cleverest of the company, will draw Water out of a Well, at her Master's command, without any other signal being given than the sound of the voice; this command being pronounced both in French and Italian. All who have witnessed her prompt obedience, have expressed themselves at once astonished and delighted at the prodigy.

The Wonderful Dog
WILL PLAY ANY GENTLEMAN AT DOMINOES THAT WILL PLAY WITH HIM

Gentleman 4d. ——Working People 2d.
Printed at the Literary Saloon, 14, Holywell-street, Strand.

A handbill advertising one of the Tower's competitors in 1832. Strange competition, certainly, but by no means the strangest.

—That a Committee be appointed to adopt measures for Inspecting the Markets and Streets of the Metropolis, the Slaughter Houses, the conduct of Coachmen, etc. etc.[*]

In fact the living arrangements Cops had set up for his charges were far better than in almost any other public animal show, but as it turned out no amount of compassion for his dumb friends was enough to secure the Menagerie's future.

For 1824 also saw rumblings that led to the birth of another great institution, one that was to have a far more lethal effect on the Menagerie than the SPCA ever did. As the SPCA began its controversial campaigns, Stamford Raffles, an oriental scholar and the founder of Singapore, was returning from the East with an idea. A dedicated amateur naturalist and collector, Raffles wanted to set up a Zoological Society, to provide 'a very different series of exhibitions to the population of [the] metropolis; namely, animals brought from every part of the globe to be applied either to some useful purpose, or as objects of scientific research, not of vulgar admiration.' (At Mr Cops's deplorable establishment, it is implied, the currency is 'vulgar admiration,' and not nearly enough serious-minded attention is being paid to scientific matters by the right kind of people.)

---

[*] It is salutary to remember that until the passing of the Factory Act in 1833 (more then a decade *later*) there was no law providing any restriction on child labor, meaning that while all this care was extended to animals, there were still five-year-old children being forced to work in textile factories or being sent up chimneys. The year 1833 would also see the belated abolition of slavery in Britain's colonies.

In the early 1790s the Jardin des Plantes had acquired the large royal collections of animals from Versailles and elsewhere, and formed a public animal collection (this development was part of the postrevolutionary nationalizing of many formerly private treasures that resulted in projects such as the founding of the Musée du Louvre). Spending time in Paris not long after this animal collection in the Jardin des Plantes was formed, Raffles had been inspired by this new institution, and hoped that London's equivalent might in time grow to be better still. Once the support had been enlisted of a number of the most eminent men of his day – scientists like Sir Humphry Davy (president of the Royal Society, chemist, inventor of the miners' lamp and soon-to-be visitor to the freshly slaughtered Chunee in his blood-drenched cell) and Cook's botanist companion Joseph Banks, as well as other notables, including the duke of Wellington – the Zoological Society of London was inaugurated with a meeting on 29 April 1826.

The Society's first act was to launch plans for a Zoological Garden on a five-acre site (about an eighth of today's site) acquired on the northern fringes of Regent's Park.* Raffles did not live to see the Garden opened in 1828 (he died in 1826, just two months after his Society's establishment). This new garden, it was hoped, would enable 'the advancement of Zoology and Animal Physiology'; rather than encouraging the 'vulgar admiration' of the public, it was to be a place to inspire scientists and those generally

---

* Then still *The* Regent's Park; the regent for whom it was named was after all still alive, though now King George IV.

well-disposed towards scientific thought. So eager was the Society to promote its experimental mandate that it held its first scientific meeting in 1827, before the Garden had even opened.* Only the *Literary Gazette* was snide about the Garden proposal, writing that 'we do not know how the inhabitants of the Regent's Park will like the lions, leopards and linxes so near their neighbourhood.'

Besides the collection itself, the new Society's facilities also included a purpose-built dissection room, where in 1829 the Garden's first orangutan was dissected by Dr Richard Owen, the assistant curator of the late John Hunter's collection, which he had spent many of the previous years cataloguing.† The collection on display in the Garden was soon fully catalogued, with 1830 seeing the publication of a detailed guidebook by their treacherous associate Edward Turner Bennett (author of *The Tower Menagerie*), who obviously knew a good thing when he saw one.

As if to emphasize the scientific nature of the enterprise, it was called, even at its earliest planning stage, a zoological garden, and not a menagerie. A zoological garden: well, it was a name deriving from the word 'zoology,' wasn't it? And 'zoology' is a good, scientific, serious, classical word, isn't it? A 'menagerie'

---

* The Society even had its own museum at its Bruton Street headquarters; contents ranged from a single common mouse to a panda, a seal and a zebra, from wolves and monkeys to a capistrated squirrel and a penciled phascogale, all stuffed, of course. In 1836 the Museum was transferred to Leicester Square where for five years it cohabited with the Hunterian Collection.

† This was necessary only because the collection's first executor, Sir Everard Home, had been publishing Hunter's work as his own and, rather tiresomely for Owen, had sought to dispose of the evidence by burning almost all of Hunter's papers.

(the word now most commonly used to describe the animals in the Tower) sounded rather self-indulgent and continental, probably French – no, it wouldn't do at all. Yes, 'The Zoological Gardens of the Zoological Society of London in The Regent's Park.' Nice ring to it. Within twenty years, it would become simply 'the zoo.'

Admission to the Garden was technically restricted to Fellows and their guests, but the general public were sufficiently excited by the idea that they sought ways of procuring tickets (Fellows were allowed to sell tickets – selectively – to guests for a shilling apiece) – so although the Fellowship numbered only about eleven hundred, the Zoo's first head keeper, James Cops[*] (no relation of Alfred that I have been able to ascertain) saw admissions for the opening seven months ring in at 30,000 and growing, with 1829 witnessing an astonishing 199,576 visitors.[†] These were the kind of numbers the Tower's Alfred Cops could only dream of. He had good reason to be worried.

Not only was Cops facing this new and energetic competition, he also found himself struggling against an antagonist closer to

---

[*] He retained the post for only about six months before being discharged for 'several acts of misconduct,' unspecified.

[†] It was not until 1847 that the Zoological Gardens – in straitened financial circumstances – began to let in anyone prepared to pay the shilling admission, but only on Mondays and Tuesdays. The price remained fixed for almost a century. Gradually the Public Days began to spread through the week, until Fellows were left with just Sundays for their exclusive use. Full (seven-day) public admission was introduced in 1957.

home, who threatened to bring the Menagerie down from within. And a formidable antagonist at that.

If Cops was a more hands-on keeper than the Menagerie had ever known before, he was cursed with a constable of the Tower who was even more extraordinarily proactive, and one who took his job far more seriously than many would have liked. Where in the past the post of constable had been given to senior public servants to keep them quiet and happy after retirement (in a post in which they were not expected actually to do anything), the new incumbent, appointed in 1826, was not a man likely to shirk his duties, and sit by idly watching the Tower and its component institutions stumble thoughtlessly along.

At the death of Lord Hastings, the post of constable had again been up for grabs, and more than one dignitary was known to be interested. Lord Londonderry, a Tory peer, asked his friend the duke of Wellington to try to secure the post for him, but the king's mind had already been made up. The post was a great honor (though salaried at a mere seven or eight hundred pounds a year), and the king felt it should be offered to the greatest and most honorable man he knew. He wrote in December to his constable-elect of 'the gratitude this country owes you. The glory of my reign is so identified with *you*, that the *one* cannot be separated from the *other*.' And after a brief correspondence, it was announced that the Iron Duke was to take charge of the Tower himself.

Arthur Wellesley, duke of Wellington, was in 1826 one of England's foremost public figures, a national hero (the Battle of Waterloo was still very much recent history) and brilliant military strategist – and soon-to-be prime minister. And this man of action *par excellence* brought his no-nonsense, businesslike approach to this new position – much to the surprise and alarm of Cops and his colleagues – determining from the outset to put the Tower in working order, eliminate waste and corruption, and emphasize its role as an important military fortress (now being run by a tried and tested military man). As such, Wellington was not impressed with the hordes of tourists swarming in through the western entrance every day, idling around, getting in the way of his garrisons, scrawling graffiti on the walls, fiddling with the arms in the Armoury, asking trivial or awkward questions of the warders and generally lowering the tone.

The duke had quite different ideas. Fearing the Tower might be a target if ever there were to be civil unrest in the capital (not in the least bit unlikely, it must be said), he wanted to strengthen its role as a military base, always one of the functions of the Tower after all; he himself was a military man, and had been given the post of constable largely on the strength of his great military successes, so a military priority should hardly surprise us. He wanted to fortify the buildings, and to use them to house a larger garrison, and the presence of the growing Menagerie beside the western entrance complicated both of these plans. The fact that Wellington had already declared an interest in the fledgling Zoological Society and its new Zoological Garden in the Regent's Park may appear – to the more cynically inclined – to have had some little to do with it too.

Besides, Wellington argued, not only were the visitors themselves a nuisance (the visitor entrance was situated right where his garrisons were trying to maneuver on and off the site), and a rapidly growing one at that, but the whole Menagerie was already enormously expensive to maintain (very true), and its costs threatened to spiral higher and higher as it grew in size and ambition. Besides, there was hardly any space into which it could grow. And anyway, how safe could it be to keep these wild animals at such close quarters with humans?

With both animal and visitor numbers soaring, and with the consequent problems of cost and crowding, Cops must have seen that the Menagerie was likely to fall victim to its own success – or at least it would if Wellington had his way, and he generally did.

It was some years before Wellington was able to begin his dismantling of the Menagerie, though. In the intervening period he'd been kept quite busy being prime minister, but in November 1830 he found himself suddenly relieved of that burden and with a lot of time on his hands.

As Wellington had guessed, and perhaps hoped, concerns about safety in the Menagerie were real and relevant. On 6 January 1830, the *Times* had run a story about Joseph Croney, a young man who was employed to clear the Menagerie of the animals' waste. No sooner had he entered the empty yard to begin his work than one of the leopards pushed open his cage door, which had not been securely shut:

> The poor fellow, seeing the perilous situation in which he was placed, made for the keeper's apartment, but before he could stir many paces, the infuriated beast sprang from his den towards him. The unfortunate Croney flew behind some

timber near him, thinking to avoid the fury of the animal, but at that moment the leopard pounced upon him, and, sticking his immense claws on either side of his neck, grasped the back of his neck with his tusks, and kept a fast hold. The poor fellow shrieked out in the most excruciating pain, and expected nothing but instant destruction, and, with the animal fastened as above described, he hobbled to the keeper's room, when, to add to his dreadful fears, he found the door fastened by a latch, and could not open it.

Two of the Menagerie's underkeepers were not far off and heard Croney's screams (and can you blame him?), and within moments they were in the yard struggling to free the unfortunate young man from the mauling he was receiving. Finding little success in coaxing the leopard away from his victim, 'one of them seized a fowling piece, and commenced beating him over the head with the but-end till they succeeded in completely stunning him [the leopard, we presume] and being no longer able to keep his hold, he dropped quite insensible, but not till the gun was broken in pieces.' Thanks to the speedy efforts of a local doctor who dressed his wounds, Croney made it more or less intact over the river to Guy's Hospital, where the principal surgeon, Mr Morgan, managed to save his life. The *Times* reports that at the time of going to press, 'although the sufferer remains in excessive agony, he is considered to be doing well.'

Wellington set about capitalizing on this incident, and upon hearing word in June of the death of the old king he took action.

King George, who had been a faithful supporter of both Cops and the new Zoological Society, was a passionate admirer of all things exotic. There was, for instance, a famous Nubian giraffe he had been given in 1827, a present from Mehemet Ali, the pasha of Egypt. The king, enchanted by this animal, had a big paddock constructed for her, and kept two Egyptian cows to serve as her wet nurses (she was only an infant); he even commissioned a portrait of her from Jacques-Laurent Agasse,* although (said the king) 'nothing could give an idea of the beauty of her eyes.'

But the animal-loving king had now died, and his brother William had no more than a passing interest in animals, and certainly no desire to become embroiled in the running of a concern like the Menagerie. So in his capacity as one of King George's executors, Wellington, acting swiftly, set in motion a plan to transfer the 150 royal animals – among them Old Martin – to the collection in Regent's Park. This proposal was reported in the *Times* on 19 August 1830 – George had been dead less than two months.

The new king, William IV, gave his approval for the dissolution of the royal component of the Menagerie in 1831, and towards the end of the year the move went ahead. The minutes of the Zoological Society Council for 21 December 1831 refer to the Council's acceptance 'of his Majesty's most generous offer . . . of the Collection of Wild Animals . . . now in the Tower.' On 29 December, the transfer was reported in the press.

Cops continued to show his own collection at the Tower for

---

* An artist who had also done pictures of a number of Exeter 'Change animals, incidentally.

some years after the departure of the royal animals, and his collection was not insignificant – over the years he had accumulated all sorts of rare and exciting species (Hudson Bay wolves and the like) – even if financial pressures meant that he too had had to sell a few of his own to the Zoological Society in October 1832. But although there was less to draw tourists to the Tower now that the king's animals had gone, Cops helped to keep visitor numbers up by halving admission prices from a shilling (an admission fee Bayley considered 'a more moderate charge than other collections that are far less worthy of public notice') to 6*d*, to compensate for the smaller show; after all, visitors must be made to feel that they were still getting good value for their money.

When Thomas Sopwith (a mining engineer from Newcastle) visited the Tower around this time, he reported finding the Menagerie 'much more confined and insignificant than I expected.' But with the exception of Sopwith it would appear that the public were still being kept happy, that the 'Wonders of Nature!' Cops was advertising still made visiting worthwhile. Constable Wellington was not pleased, however. Even a scaled-down public was still too much public for his liking, and there were still the issues of safety and hygiene and maintenance cost. It was just a nuisance, and he wanted it out.

Wellington's excuse to get rid of the whole thing once and for all didn't materialize until a few years later, but when it came it was decisive. First, on Tuesday, 29 April 1834, a report appeared in the *Times* about the unfortunate escape two days previously of a 'large and furious wolf,' which had managed to get out of his den 'during the hours of divine service':

The animal . . . was making its way across the drawbridge towards the interior of the Tower, when Baldwin, the gatekeeper of the drawbridge gate, perceiving his approach, closed the wicket [gate], which, as usual during church hours, was the only part of it opened. The wolf, finding his progress impeded, turned round and seized a small terrier dog, belonging to Sergeant Cropper, that had followed him. The poor dog, after receiving a severe shaking, by some means got away and proceeded up a flight of stairs towards the room of its owner. The wolf followed close behind, and rushed into the apartment, close at his heels. The terror of Mrs Cropper, the sergeant's wife, and her two children, who were in the room at the time, on seeing the infuriated animal, may be more easily conceived than described; but the wolf was so intent on the object of his pursuit, that he fortunately did not take the slightest notice of anything else, and having seized the poor dog a second time, gave Mrs Cropper and her children an opportunity of leaving the room unhurt, and closing the door.

After no little struggle the wolf was recaptured by Cops's assistant Benjamin Poulter and his colleagues. When quizzed about how he could possibly have been allowed to escape, the keepers excused themselves, explaining that 'during their absence there were some pieces of bread in the yard opposite to his cage, and he by some extraordinary effort forced himself out between the bars in front, and having devoured the bread was proceeding, as has been before stated, to the interior of the Tower.'

There is no record of what became of the terrier, but descriptions of the wolf's mood suggest that, alas, he might not have made it. And although no one (apart from said martyred terrier) was injured in this incident, the following year saw a more serious accident, the one that probably made all the difference.

In August 1835, a member of Wellington's highly prized garrison, one Ensign Seymour (of the '3rd Guards'), had his leg bitten by one of Cops's monkeys, and had to be 'consigned for a considerable time to his chamber.' This happened while Seymour was taking a shortcut through the animals' enclosure, where he should not have been (some might say he had only himself to blame), but this detail wasn't enough to stay Wellington from coming down on the Tower Menagerie with his usual vigor and determination.

Earlier that month the new king had received a magnificent array of gifts from the king of Oudh (a frontier kingdom in northeastern India), and had decided not to entrust them to Cops. The story was reported in the *Times* on 8 August, the day after the animals' arrival at the West India Docks:

> There are . . . two elephants, two Arabian horses, and two
> dwarf buffaloes. The elephants, which are male and female, are
> of a particularly small breed, and not yet full grown, being only
> in their eleventh year. They are accompanied by attendants,
> natives of the East Indies, who are clothed in oriental dresses of
> scarlet and gold. On Thursday night the male elephant was
> moved to Mr Cross' establishment, the Surrey Zoological-
> gardens, and last night the female was removed to the

Zoological-gardens in the Regent's-park, *in obedience to the express commands of His Majesty*. We understand that the Arabian horses will forthwith be moved to Windsor [my italics].

Cops must have known what this meant. Nonetheless he continued to fight to keep his collection open, writing to Major Elrington (the governor of the Tower) and Wellington, but to no avail. His resistance is understandable; although he must have seen the benefits to the animals of the setup in the Regent's Park, he must too have felt a strong attachment to his job and to the animals themselves – those currently still at the Tower were after all his own private collection, and Wellington was trying to destroy everything Cops had worked so hard to build up, all for reasons that must have seemed to him to be largely spurious and self-serving. Besides, to the Menagerie's credit it had been centuries since admission had been limited to members of the elite; and yet now these animals the public had come to love would be hidden away behind the walls of the ZSL's members-only garden. Surely this could not be a good thing? But against a man like Wellington there was nothing Cops could do about it.

By the end of the month it was all over. The Iron Duke had finally lost patience. His letter to the major is curt and unambiguous. His tone allows no room for debate. 'The King is determined that wild beasts shall not be kept there. Mr Cops had better dispose of his.'

On 27 August, Cops had to acknowledge that he had finally lost the battle. He wrote to Elrington, 'I have arranged that his

Majesty's wishes should be obeyed and that the Exhibition should be closed tomorrow.'

On 12 October, the people of London were held spellbound by the beautiful passage of Halley's comet, last seen in 1758, the year Linnaeus had published that important edition of *Systema Naturae*, three generations earlier.

And now, on 29 October, the last page of the *Times* carried a tiny story (bottom lefthand corner), beginning 'The Tower of London Menagery, this ancient exhibition, no longer exists.'

The report explained that the closure was forced upon the Tower partly by the 'unwholesome state of the atmosphere' that – apparently – had killed the old lion (consumption, or so they said). Meanwhile Mr Cops, it is confirmed, 'holds the situation of keeper by patent,' so 'although the exhibition no longer exists, he retains his house, with a salary of 11s a day.'

> A few weeks since the above remnants [the bear, the monkeys and birds] were disposed of to an American gentleman, and exported to that country. Last week the materials which formed the dens &c., were sold, broken up, and conveyed away.

In his remaining decades at the Lion House, Cops would continue to trade, or at least to help visiting Americans to buy for their collections. On occasion these visitors would even stay in Cops's house, and Benjamin Franklin Brown was one of these. He was almost certainly the 'American gentleman' who bought Cops's last animals; in 1841 he would marry Cops's daughter Mary.

*

The large majority of the collection had already been given or sold to the Zoological Society, of course; but there was another organization – newer even than that – just across the water in Ireland. And the Zoological Society of Dublin wanted a little of this huge animal windfall for themselves.

The Zoological Society of Dublin had been founded in 1830 on the model of the London Society, as subsequently were a number of zoos across the world. At its very first meeting it had initiated plans to 'form a collection of Living Animals on the plan of the Zoological Society of London,' to whom it accordingly wrote, 'to ascertain what Animals the London Zoological Society plan to give this Society.'

A year later another letter was received at Regent's Park, requesting any 'such Animals as they can spare or have duplicates of,' and in November 1832 a reminder that (apparently) His Majesty's animals had been presented to London only 'with an intimation of His Majesty's desire that such duplicates as the London Society could spare shall be given to our Society.' Regent's Park succumbed to the pressure, and as a gesture of goodwill speedily dispatched 'several valuable animals' to the keepers in Dublin; His Majesty himself sent a gift of a leopard, a hyena and a wolf directly from the royal collection.

Like Regent's Park, the new Dublin zoo aimed at a level of scientific professionalism that the old animal showmen at the Tower would have had little interest in. They began by instituting 'Transaction Books,' a page a week, recording as systematically as they possibly could which animals had arrived and whence purchased (on the IN page), and on the facing page (OUT) which ones had died and of what cause (and to whom the cadavers had then been sold) – something no one at the Tower ever seems to have thought of recording. But though their intentions were doubtless noble, one has to wonder, reading these books, quite how useful the information they collected can possibly have been. Most of the causes of death are predictable – old age, consumption – but in their attempts to be more specific, to provide more varied data, the keepers clearly found their powers of diagnosis rather taxed. An early death was blamed on a 'disease of the head,' and this poor creature was followed quickly to its grave by an alligator who had died of 'Exhaustion.' The OUT page for the week ending 18 August 1836 reads:

Jackal	—	Decline
Grey parrot	—	Fits
Angora cat	—	Killed by the Dingo

The following week two birds died 'from fright.' A little later a summer duck was drowned, a number of birds were 'Killed and eaten by rats' (following which a Virginia quail died 'Pining after its companion'), and a green parakeet suffocated. Besides these there were animals killed by swans, by Australian dogs, by jackals; a black vulture 'Killed itself' and several squirrels 'Killed each other.' It cannot have been a pretty sight. The conscientious Mr Cops would not have been impressed.

In 1838, at the start of Queen Victoria's long reign, Old Martin died in his new home. His death was reported in the press, and word must have reached his former keeper, Cops, still living at his old house in the Tower. Cops himself lived on.

The year 1852 saw the demolition of the Lion Tower, just

beside the house where Cops was still living. It also saw the death of the duke of Wellington. As befitted a man of his position a state funeral was held for him, a very grand and solemn affair, and he was buried with much ceremony in St Paul's Cathedral. And while the nation was preoccupied with this event, the authorities in the Tower had their minds on another matter — trying to predict how long they would have to accommodate Cops on their site (for the purposes of their building development plans, presumably). They had recently estimated that he could be reasonably expected to live another thirteen years and a quarter.

They did not have to wait quite so long for the old keeper to die, however, for he obliged prematurely, on 21 March of the very next year. Within weeks of his death, arrangements were being made by the Tower authorities for his younger daughter Sarah and her husband to be removed from the property. Cops had been guaranteed the house during his lifetime, but the Tower officials would be damned if they would let such an abuse continue even a month longer if they could help it.

On 23 September the Lion House itself was auctioned off, its disparate parts bought up to be used as building materials, and what remained was finally pulled down. For almost a year it had been all that was left of the Great Menagerie, and now it too was gone.

It was not forgotten, however. In 1857, four years after Cops's death, and more than two decades after the last animals had been transferred out of the old Tower to young London Zoo, invitations were issued to a very special ceremony. One 'Percy B. Greville' requested that visitors to the Tower report to the 'White Gate,' there to hand in their highly prized invitations and be shown in to witness the ceremony. When the important guests arrived, they found themselves circling the Tower, in search of this 'White Gate,' utterly bewildered; and it's no wonder they were having trouble, since no such gate has ever existed at the Tower. The invitation read:

> Please to Admit the Bearer and Friend,
> to view the
> ANNUAL CEREMONY
> of Washing the Lions

It was April the first.

Epilogue

More than a century and a half has passed since the last royal animals were moved out of the Tower to the new gardens in the Regent's Park; almost eight centuries since the first animals were brought back to England from foreign parts and housed in the Tower. The play of international relations has changed sufficiently over those centuries that we would hardly expect Queen Elizabeth II and her family to be burdened these days as Henry III was with leopards, polar bears and elephants, those awkward tokens of friendship from miscellaneous foreign powers hoping to impress. And yet the truth is that at least this much hasn't changed at all. In 1961, the young Prince Andrew received a baby crocodile as a gift from Gambia. Four years later the people of Germany sent his mother the Queen a canary. Brazil dispatched a load of sloths and jaguars in 1968, then yet more sloths, an anteater and an armadillo in 1976. And what was she to do with them? All these animals made their way to London Zoo, of course, where they lived out their lives before an admiring public, as did the beavers brought over for the Queen from Canada, the elephant from Cameroon, the giant turtles from the Seychelles, the Liberian pygmy hippos . . .

And what of the Tower itself? Well, whatever the 'Washing the Lions' advertisements may suggest, there is no longer a zoo at the

Tower of London. There is still a collection of ravens quartered beside the Wakefield Tower, but although they have been at the Tower for centuries there is nothing to link them directly to the once famous Royal Menagerie. These birds provide some continuity, nonetheless, as a three-century-old legend says that when the ravens leave the Tower some terrible evil will befall the country – the White Tower will crumble, and the kingdom will crumble with it. On certain days visitors to the Tower are surprised to espy an Indian blackbuck antelope prancing happily around the dry moat where he is occasionally put out to graze. He is the mascot of the Royal Regiment of Fusiliers, whose headquarters are at the Tower, and the Regiment has named him Bobby. These – and the small open foundations of the Lion Tower to be seen at the tourist entrance – are the only echoes that remain on-site of the Menagerie in the Tower. With one possible exception.

About two centuries ago it was reported that among the many ghosts haunting the Tower was that of a bear that had died there; in one reported sighting this phantom appeared from under a door in the Martin Tower and startled a soldier on duty, who promptly keeled over and died from the shock. As far as I have been able to establish, this animal apparition has not been seen since, I'm sorry to say, and one has to wonder if he is still around. But I do hope so.

A Note on Sources

Although I don't think this is a book that would benefit from pages and pages of detailed source-notes, there are a few references I should include, both in order to acknowledge debts and to give some suggestions for further reading. Needless to say if any reader has queries about particular sources I'd be happy to answer them.

For general Tower-related matters, the classic account of its history is Derek Wilson's *The Tower of London: A Thousand Years*, first published in 1978 but revised and reissued a few years ago. Gustave Loisel's three-volume *Histoire des ménageries de l'antiquité à nos jours*, published in 1912, is still the most comprehensive work on the long history of animal collections around the world, though to my knowledge it has never been updated. On public exhibitions, freak shows and the like, Richard D. Altick's book *The Shows of London* is a marvelous read – widely researched, generously illustrated and full of delightful (and sometimes gruesome) detail. Much of the material I have used in my section on Chunee at the start of chapter 8 came from this source. I am also indebted to the work of Professor Harriet Ritvo, in particular her landmark study of animal-human relations in the nineteenth century, *The Animal Estate*.

On the matter of our perceptions of animals and our sense of their (and our) place in the world, by far the best book is Keith Thomas's exemplary *Man and the Natural World*. Covering a full three centuries of this rich subject, it is an ambitious, masterly piece of research and writing; since its publication two decades ago it has not been superseded, nor do I see that happening any time soon.

Much original research into the structure and workings of the Menagerie was carried out by the keeper of Tower history, Dr Geoffrey Parnell, for the Tower's exhibition on this subject. Parnell's accompanying guidebook introduced me to several details and quotations I might not have found elsewhere.

Thanks to Graham Keevill for permission to quote from the Oxford Archaeological Unit report on the excavations of the Lion Tower on page 35; and to John Cleese for permission to quote from the screenplay to *Fierce Creatures* (Fish Productions, 1997) on page 74. The epigraph to chapter 2 is taken from *The Name of the Rose* by Umberto Eco, published by Secker & Warburg, and is used by permission of the Random House Group Ltd. Finally, the Antonia Fraser quotation on page 102 is taken from *King James* (Weidenfeld & Nicolson, 1974), and is reproduced by kind permission of the author.

Index

Page numbers in *italic* refer to the illustrations in the text.

Index

art, animals in, 50–62, 52, 55, 58, 60, 171
Ashmole, Elias, 136–7
Ashmolean Museum, Oxford, 137–8 and n.
Asia, 133
Astrakhan, 136
Atlantic Ocean, 67, 80–1
Australia, 184
aviary, 208, 216
Aztecs, 68–9

baboons, 180, 215
Bacon, Francis, 99–100
Bainbridge, Beryl, 156n.
Banks, Joseph, 134, 166, 184, 204, 227
Bayley, John, 208, 235
Beagle, HMS, 185
bears: brown bears, 85–6; bear-baiting, 86, 87, 88–92, 113–14, 224; Old Martin, 196–7, 207, 234, 241; housed with hyenas, 217–18; ghost of, 246; *see also* polar bears
beavers, 107, 245
Beethoven, Ludwig van, 2n.
Belgium, 131
Belle Sauvage inn, 137n., 140 and n.
Bengal, nabob of, 183
Bennett, Edward Turner, 209–16, 221, 228
Bentham, Jeremy, 186, 189
Berkeley Castle, 44
bestiaries, 37, 38–41, 50, 65, 84, 173

Bethlehem Royal Hospital (Bedlam), 146–7 and n., 153, 172–3
Bible, 58, 65, 84, 100
Bigod, Hugh, 30, 33
Billewicz, Teodor, 102
Birdcage Walk, 136n.
black bears, 217
Black Death, 62, 108
Blackwood, Gary, 156n.
Blake, William, 61, 162n.
Blenheim Palace, Oxfordshire, 14, 172
Blood, Colonel, 123, 173
boa constrictors, 218–19 and n.
Boleyn, Anne, 27, 49, 104
Borges, Jorge Luis, 187
Botanic Gardens, Oxford, 131
Botton, William de, 13, 19, 28–9, 74, 219
Bounde, William, 45, 46
Bowyer, Robert le, 46
Brackenbury, Sir Robert, 29, 77
Branston, Mr (engraver), 212
Braun and Hogenberg, 88, 90–1
Bray, Henry de, 49
Brazil, 245
British Empire, 148, 182–3
British Museum, 129
Brocas, Martin, 138
Brome, Richard, 69–72
Brown, Benjamin Franklin, 239
Brown, Lancelot, 'Capability,' 14, 172
brown bears, 85–6
Brussels, 133
Buck, Sir George, 128

Index

Index

Index

Index